MODERN WORLD LEADERS

Hosni Mubarak

MODERN WORLD LEADERS

MODERN WORLD LEADERS

Hosni Mubarak

Susan Muaddi Darraj

CHELSEA HOUSE
PUBLISHERS
An imprint of Infobase Publishing

Hosni Mubarak

Chelsea House
An imprint of Infobase Publishing
132 West 31st Street
New York, NY 10001

ISBN-10: 0-7910-9280-1
ISBN-13: 978-0-7910-9280-4

Library of Congress Cataloging-in-Publication Data

Darraj, Susan Muaddi.
  Hosni Mubarak / Susan Muaddi Darraj.
    p. cm. — (Modern world leaders)
  Includes bibliographical references and index.
  ISBN 0-7910-9280-1 (hardcover)
  1. Mubarak, Muhammad Hosni, 1928– Juvenile literature. 2. Presidents—Egypt—Biography—Juvenile literature. 3. Egypt—Politics and government—1981—Juvenile literature. I. Title. DT107.87D37 2007
  962.05'5092—dc22   2006032696

Text design by Erik Lindstrom
Cover design by Takeshi Takahashi

Printed in the United States of America

Bang FOF 10 9 8 7 6 5 4 3 2 1

This book is printed on acid-free paper.

All links and Web addresses were checked and verified to be correct at the time of publication. Because of the dynamic nature of the Web, some addresses and links may have changed since publication and may no longer be valid.

TABLE OF CONTENTS

ARTHUR M. SCHLESINGER, JR.

On Leadership

Leadership, it may be said, is really what makes the world go round. Love no doubt smoothes the passage; but love is a private transaction between consenting adults. Leadership is a public transaction with history. The idea of leadership affirms the capacity of individuals to move, inspire, and mobilize masses of people so that they act together in pursuit of an end. Sometimes leadership serves good purposes, sometimes bad; but whether the end is benign or evil, great leaders are those men and women who leave their personal stamp on history.

Now, the very concept of leadership implies the proposition that individuals can make a difference. This proposition has never been universally accepted. From classical times to the present day, eminent thinkers have regarded individuals as no more than the agents and pawns of larger forces, whether the gods and goddesses of the ancient world or, in the modern era, race, class, nation, the dialectic, the will of the people, the spirit of the times, history itself. Against such forces, the individual dwindles into insignificance.

So contends the thesis of historical determinism. Tolstoy's great novel *War and Peace* offers a famous statement of the case. Why, Tolstoy asked, did millions of men in the Napoleonic Wars, denying their human feelings and their common sense, move back and forth across Europe slaughtering their fellows? "The war," Tolstoy answered, "was bound to happen simply because it was bound to happen." All prior history determined it. As for leaders, they, Tolstoy said, "are but the labels that serve to give a name to an end and, like labels, they have the least possible connection with the event." The greater the leader, "the more conspicuous the inevitability and the predestination of every act he commits." The leader, said Tolstoy, is "the slave of history."

Determinism takes many forms. Marxism is the determinism of class. Nazism the determinism of race. But the idea of men and women as the slaves of history runs athwart the deepest human instincts. Rigid determinism abolishes the idea of human freedom—the assumption of free choice that underlies every move we make, every word we speak, every thought we think. It abolishes the idea of human responsibility, since it is manifestly unfair to reward or punish people for actions that are by definition beyond their control. No one can live consistently by any deterministic creed. The Marxist states prove this themselves by their extreme susceptibility to the cult of leadership.

More than that, history refutes the idea that individuals make no difference. In December 1931, a British politician crossing Fifth Avenue in New York City between 76th and 77th streets around 10:30 P.M. looked in the wrong direction and was knocked down by an automobile—a moment, he later recalled, of a man aghast, a world aglare: "I do not understand why I was not broken like an eggshell or squashed like a gooseberry." Fourteen months later an American politician, sitting in an open car in Miami, Florida, was fired on by an assassin; the man beside him was hit. Those who believe that individuals make no difference to history might well ponder whether the next two decades would have been the same had Mario Constasino's car killed Winston Churchill in 1931 and Giuseppe Zangara's bullet killed Franklin Roosevelt in 1933. Suppose, in addition, that Lenin had died of typhus in Siberia in 1895 and that Hitler had been killed on the western front in 1916. What would the twentieth century have looked like now?

For better or for worse, individuals do make a difference. "The notion that a people can run itself and its affairs anonymously," wrote the philosopher William James, "is now well known to be the silliest of absurdities. Mankind does nothing save through initiatives on the part of inventors, great or small, and imitation by the rest of us—these are the sole factors in human progress. Individuals of genius show the way, and set the patterns, which common people then adopt and follow."

Leadership, James suggests, means leadership in thought as well as in action. In the long run, leaders in thought may well make the greater difference to the world. "The ideas of economists and political philosophers, both when they are right and when they are wrong," wrote John Maynard Keynes, "are more powerful than is commonly understood. Indeed the world is ruled by little else. Practical men, who believe themselves to be quite exempt from any intellectual influences, are usually the slaves of some defunct economist. . . . The power of vested interests is vastly exaggerated compared with the gradual encroachment of ideas."

But, as Woodrow Wilson once said, "Those only are leaders of men, in the general eye, who lead in action. . . . It is at their hands that new thought gets its translation into the crude language of deeds." Leaders in thought often invent in solitude and obscurity, leaving to later generations the tasks of imitation. Leaders in action—the leaders portrayed in this series—have to be effective in their own time.

And they cannot be effective by themselves. They must act in response to the rhythms of their age. Their genius must be adapted, in a phrase from William James, "to the receptivities of the moment." Leaders are useless without followers. "There goes the mob," said the French politician, hearing a clamor in the streets. "I am their leader. I must follow them." Great leaders turn the inchoate emotions of the mob to purposes of their own. They seize on the opportunities of their time, the hopes, fears, frustrations, crises, potentialities. They succeed when events have prepared the way for them, when the community is awaiting to be aroused, when they can provide the clarifying and organizing ideas. Leadership completes the circuit between the individual and the mass and thereby alters history.

It may alter history for better or for worse. Leaders have been responsible for the most extravagant follies and most monstrous crimes that have beset suffering humanity. They have also been vital in such gains as humanity has made in individual freedom, religious and racial tolerance, social justice, and respect for human rights.

There is no sure way to tell in advance who is going to lead for good and who for evil. But a glance at the gallery of men and women in MODERN WORLD LEADERS suggests some useful tests.

One test is this: Do leaders lead by force or by persuasion? By command or by consent? Through most of history leadership was exercised by the divine right of authority. The duty of followers was to defer and to obey. "Theirs not to reason why/Theirs but to do and die." On occasion, as with the so-called enlightened despots of the eighteenth century in Europe, absolutist leadership was animated by humane purposes. More often, absolutism nourished the passion for domination, land, gold, and conquest and resulted in tyranny.

The great revolution of modern times has been the revolution of equality. "Perhaps no form of government," wrote the British historian James Bryce in his study of the United States, *The American Commonwealth*, "needs great leaders so much as democracy." The idea that all people should be equal in their legal condition has undermined the old structure of authority, hierarchy, and deference. The revolution of equality has had two contrary effects on the nature of leadership. For equality, as Alexis de Tocqueville pointed out in his great study *Democracy in America*, might mean equality in servitude as well as equality in freedom.

"I know of only two methods of establishing equality in the political world," Tocqueville wrote. "Rights must be given to every citizen, or none at all to anyone . . . save one, who is the master of all." There was no middle ground "between the sovereignty of all and the absolute power of one man." In his astonishing prediction of twentieth-century totalitarian dictatorship, Tocqueville explained how the revolution of equality could lead to the *Führerprinzip* and more terrible absolutism than the world had ever known.

But when rights are given to every citizen and the sovereignty of all is established, the problem of leadership takes a new form, becomes more exacting than ever before. It is easy to issue commands and enforce them by the rope and the stake, the concentration camp and the *gulag*. It is much harder to use argument and achievement to overcome opposition and win consent. The Founding Fathers of the United States understood the difficulty. They believed that history had given them the opportunity to decide, as Alexander Hamilton wrote in the first Federalist Paper, whether men are indeed capable of basing government on "reflection and choice, or whether they are forever destined to depend . . . on accident and force."

Government by reflection and choice called for a new style of leadership and a new quality of followership. It required leaders to be responsive to popular concerns, and it required followers to be active and informed participants in the process. Democracy does not eliminate emotion from politics; sometimes it fosters demagoguery; but it is confident that, as the greatest of democratic leaders put it, you cannot fool all of the people all of the time. It measures leadership by results and retires those who overreach or falter or fail.

It is true that in the long run despots are measured by results too. But they can postpone the day of judgment, sometimes indefinitely, and in the meantime they can do infinite harm. It is also true that democracy is no guarantee of virtue and intelligence in government, for the voice of the people is not necessarily the voice of God. But democracy, by assuring the right of opposition, offers built-in resistance to the evils inherent in absolutism. As the theologian Reinhold Niebuhr summed it up, "Man's capacity for justice makes democracy possible, but man's inclination to justice makes democracy necessary."

A second test for leadership is the end for which power is sought. When leaders have as their goal the supremacy of a master race or the promotion of totalitarian revolution or the acquisition and exploitation of colonies or the protection of greed and privilege or the preservation of personal power, it is likely that their leadership will do little to advance the cause of humanity. When their goal is the abolition of slavery, the liberation of women, the enlargement of opportunity for the poor and powerless, the extension of equal rights to racial minorities, the defense of the freedoms of expression and opposition, it is likely that their leadership will increase the sum of human liberty and welfare.

Leaders have done great harm to the world. They have also conferred great benefits. You will find both sorts in this series. Even "good" leaders must be regarded with a certain wariness. Leaders are not demigods; they put on their trousers one leg after another just like ordinary mortals. No leader is infallible, and every leader needs to be reminded of this at regular intervals. Irreverence irritates leaders but is their salvation. Unquestioning submission corrupts leaders and demeans followers. Making a cult of a leader is always a mistake. Fortunately hero worship generates its own antidote. "Every hero," said Emerson, "becomes a bore at last."

The single benefit the great leaders confer is to embolden the rest of us to live according to our own best selves, to be active, insistent, and resolute in affirming our own sense of things. For great leaders attest to the reality of human freedom against the supposed inevitabilities of history. And they attest to the wisdom and power that may lie within the most unlikely of us, which is why Abraham Lincoln remains the supreme example of great leadership. A great leader, said Emerson, exhibits new possibilities to all humanity. "We feed on genius. . . . Great men exist that there may be greater men."

Great leaders, in short, justify themselves by emancipating and empowering their followers. So humanity struggles to master its destiny, remembering with Alexis de Tocqueville: "It is true that around every man a fatal circle is traced beyond which he cannot pass; but within the wide verge of that circle he is powerful and free; as it is with man, so with communities." ●

1

Killing at Queen Hatsheput's Temple

NOVEMBER 17, 1997, WAS A TYPICAL AUTUMN DAY IN LUXOR, EGYPT. The ancient city, located in the country's southeast region, on the bank of the Nile River, attracts roughly 2 million tourists a year. The site, which sits on part of what was once the ancient city of Thebes, features some of Egypt's greatest archaeological wonders, including the Temple of Amon, built by Pharaoh Amenhotep III, and the famous Temple of Queen Hatsheput, the first female pharaoh. The temple is cut into the side of a mountain and is in remarkably good condition. Its predominant architectural feature is a series of three levels, each marked by several pillars. In the center is a ramp that connects the levels and a path that leads the visitor directly to the queen's tomb.

That fall day, a tour bus filled with Swiss, Japanese, German, British, and French sightseers made its way toward

Coffins holding 36 bodies line the hangar in the Zurich airport after arriving from Cairo, Egypt. In November 1997, members of the al-Gamaa al-Islamiyya, an Islamic militant organization killed 60 people at the Hatshepsut temple in Luxor, Egypt. The Islamic extremists wanted to overthrow the government and set up an Islamic-based regime.

the majestic Temple of Queen Hatsheput. Suddenly, gunmen stepped out from behind the ruins and fired on the vehicle. A hijacking attempt was underway. The six gunmen seized control of the bus, driving it and its terrified passengers to the temple site. It is unclear whether the hijackers planned to hold the tourists hostage and demand a ransom or kill them. The incident ended in a horrific massacre at the temple, during which the gunmen killed more than 60 people. One woman survived by pretending to be dead, hiding underneath the bodies of others who had been shot. "They shot everyone in the arms and legs. Then they killed everyone who was still alive with a shot to the head," recalled the victim in an article on CNN.com.

Shortly before the massacre, the Egyptian police had received word of the hijacking and sent a fleet of officers to the temple site. A gun battle broke out between the police and the hijackers. By the time the smoke cleared, more than 70 people—tourists, police, and hijackers—lay dead.

Egyptian president Hosni Mubarak rushed to Luxor's ancient ruins as the world learned of the attack and recoiled from the shock. Already unpopular in many Egyptian circles, Mubarak was now in a very bad political position. An organization known as al-Gamaa al-Islamiyya (The Islamic Group) claimed responsibility for the attack. This group had long posed a threat to Mubarak's power, and it was determined to overthrow the administration and to install a governmental system based on traditional Islamic law.

There had been other attacks on tourists by those trying indirectly to target Mubarak's government. On September 18, 1997, two months before the massacre at Queen Hatsheput's temple, Islamic militants sympathetic to the cause of al-Gamaa al-Islamiyya and other groups with similar agendas fired on a bus in the Egyptian capital of Cairo. The bus, carrying mostly German tourists, was parked near the Egyptian Museum at Tahrir Square, one of Cairo's busiest and most crowded areas. The terrorists walked calmly up to the bus and then suddenly pulled their weapons and fired at the tourists seated inside. They fired for several minutes, and the bus eventually burst into flames as panicked bystanders fled for their safety. The attack killed nine Germans and their Egyptian driver.

Another attack had taken place on April 18, 1996. Four men in a white van pulled up outside the Europa Hotel in Cairo and opened fire on the crowd standing outside. Seventeen travelers from Greece and their Egyptian tour guide were killed. The tourists had been on an Easter holiday vacation, visiting the Christian holy sites in the Middle East; they

British tourists line up at the Luxor airport to flee the country after the terrorist attack at the ancient Hatshepsut temple. Six gunmen opened fire on the highly popular tourist attraction. Approximately 58 of the more than 60 people who were killed in the massacre were foreigners.

had just arrived from Jerusalem and were on their way to visit Alexandria. On December 27, 1993, an attack had taken place in Cairo in which gunmen injured 15 people—seven Austrians and eight Egyptians—by firing on and throwing a bomb at their tour bus.

The strategy of the militants was clear: damage the Mubarak government's power and reputation by attacking foreigners who visited Egypt. Because the country depends heavily on the enormous revenue generated by the tourist industry, hurting that economic base would weaken the government. Indeed, after the massacre at Queen Hatsheput's temple in Luxor, several foreign governments warned their citizens against traveling to Egypt. According to the BBC, after the attack, for example, the Japanese ambassador to Cairo immediately said: "I know at least three Japanese have been killed and one seriously injured. We are trying to account for the others. Until the whole picture is known I am advising Japanese tourists not to travel [to Egypt]." Switzerland's government also issued a travel advisory to Swiss tourists and flew its remaining citizens in Egypt back home. Major travel companies canceled tours to Egypt, costing the country countless dollars in lost revenue.

Speaking from Luxor, Mubarak did what he could to calm the situation and quell the panic. "This could happen anywhere in the world. We are very sorry," he said in a statement to the media. "Such people who kill human beings are not Muslims, Christians, or Jews . . . they are criminals." He ordered tighter security measures, including assigning more police to tourist sites and installing a close patrolling of the Nile River, which is a major artery of transportation. However, Mubarak's struggle with Islamic fundamentalist groups was only one threat to his power base, and with al-Gamaa al-Islamiyya promising that the Luxor massacre was only the beginning, the road to the future for Mubarak—and Egypt—would be obstructed with challenges.

2

Pharaonic Egypt

EGYPT IS ONE OF THE MOST IMPORTANT COUNTRIES IN THE MIDDLE EAST and Africa. Geographically located in the northeast corner of Africa, it connects the continent to Asia. Thus, Egypt has historically served as a passageway between the two landmasses. Due to its close location to Europe, it has always been a major Mediterranean port as well. Unfortunately, Egypt's location and wealth of resources have also made it the subject of numerous conquests by foreign invaders.

Its last rulers to come from native Egypt, before the modern era, were the pharaohs. Indeed, the legacy of the pharaonic era of Egypt continues to shape and influence the identity of Egyptians today. Before discussing the era of the pharaohs, it is essential to relate the importance of Egypt's single greatest resource: the Nile River.

According to Glenn Perry's *The History of Egypt*, the historian Herodotus once wrote: "Egypt is the gift of the Nile."

Egypt's most prized natural resource, the Nile River, is one of the longest rivers in the world. Since the majority of land in Egypt is desert, the fertile area surrounding the Nile has provided life support for its inhabitants throughout the years. Not only does the Nile provide rich soil for maximum crop production, it also serves as highway for transportation and trade.

This is a telling statement, and one whose meaning cannot be underestimated. Indeed, most of Egypt is a desert, but the land on either side of the Nile River is incredibly fertile and rich in agricultural potential. For centuries, people have redirected the Nile's waters to fortify the soil of otherwise useless land to grow crops. In fact, Egypt is the only country in the world in which 100% of the agricultural land is irrigated. The Nile serves as Egypt's most important physical attribute, and the reason for its survival over the ages.

A wonderful story exists in local Arab folklore about the Nile. According to legend, when the world was created, God told his people that he would bestow upon them a blessing, which they could choose, but that this blessing would also prove to be a curse. The inhabitants of the Arabian Peninsula desired freedom, so God granted them vast stretches of desert in which to live, where they could not be disturbed. However, they also were destined to live in poverty. The people of Syria desired intelligence, and so they were endowed with cleverness and knowledge; however, they constantly bickered with one another and with their neighbors. The Egyptians asked God for an abundance of food, so God gave them the Nile River, whose waters and annual flood left rich, fertile soil in its wake. However, because of this divine blessing, their curse was to be the envy of other nations and to be conquered by them.

The legend was prophetic: from 332 B.C. to A.D. 1952, a span of more than 2,200 years, foreigners (not native to Egypt) ruled the land. The original rulers who were of native Egyptian origin were, of course, the ancient pharaohs. The greatest of these includes Ramses II, the great peacemaker, who ruled from 1290 to 1224 B.C., and Tutankhamen, the boy king who ruled Egypt from 1334 to 1325 B.C. and whose tomb was discovered in A.D. 1922.

After the pharaohs, many others ruled Egypt, including the Nubians and the Assyrians. The Persians controlled the country in 525 B.C., but they were ousted by Alexander the Great, who conquered Egypt in 331 B.C. His conquest was not a difficult one, as the Egyptian people hated living under Persian rule. They knew of Alexander's greatness and literally welcomed him to Egypt; they even named him their new pharaoh. Fascinated with the history of the land, he toured it and spent much time there, even ordering a city to be built and named after himself at the mouth of the Nile. Though many cities across Asia and the Middle East were named after the famous leader, Alexandria in Egypt is the only one that remains today.

Upon his death in 323 B.C., Alexander's general Pompey assumed control of Egypt. Thus, a series of Greek rulers dominated Egyptian government for the next several centuries. Over

The Temple of Abu Simbel consists of two ancient rock temples carved out of a mountainside. Pharoah Ramses II, who reigned during the thirteenth century for 67 years, commissioned this grand monument. The four seated statues are approximately 65.6 feet (20 meters) high. The statues between their ankles are life-size.

time, these Greek rulers adopted some of the customs of the former elite, the pharaohs, but also retained many of their own Greek traditions. The Greek rulers generally did not mix with the native population; they kept their Greek bloodline separate and distinct from that of the people they ruled. In fact, the Mediterranean coastal city of Alexandria, their capital, was quite un-Egyptian in its character. Alexandrians spoke Greek and even dressed like Greeks. Over the years, nevertheless, the Greek kings and queens adopted more and more of the

Egyptian culture and blended its elements with their own; for example, this blending was especially noted in their style of dress, their building architecture, and their adoption of some local gods.

The most famous of these Greek rulers was the last: Cleopatra VII, who married the Roman conqueror Julius Caesar in hopes of gaining independence for Egypt, which had become essentially part of the vast Roman Empire. After Caesar's death, she married his general Marc Antony, who advocated her cause, but their attempt to liberate Egypt was defeated by Augustus, Caesar's nephew, in 30 B.C. The pharaohs were ousted from power, and Egypt—and all its resources—came fully under the control of the Roman Empire. The country languished under Roman rule until A.D. 632.

In that decade, a new empirical power quickly spread across the region: the Islamic army. The Muslims, who originated in what is now Saudi Arabia, preached a new monotheistic religion that saw itself as the successor to and outgrowth of Judaism and Christianity. In the year A.D. 610, Muhammad—the major prophet of Islam—claimed to have visions from God. He began preaching the message of God and soon gathered a large following. In the year 622, Muhammad and his followers made the *hijira*, the journey from Mecca to Medina, where they went to flee persecution. In 630, the Muslim army, under Muhammad, captured Mecca. The people converted to Islam and the tribes of the Arabian Peninsula swore their allegiance to Muhammad.

The message of Islam, which means "submission" (as in submission to God's will) was simple and featured five "pillars" that Muslims had to do: 1) believe that there is no god but God (Allah), and that Muhammad is his prophet; 2) pray five times a day; 3) give a percentage of their annual income to the poor and needy; 4) fast during the holy month of Ramadan as a means of self-purification; and 5) make a pilgrimage to Mecca, if they were able to, at least once in their lives.

At the time that the Muslim army made its way to Egypt in 632, Egypt was largely a Christian land. When the Roman Empire had become Christianized under Emperor Constantine in the early fourth century A.D., the Egyptian people had largely adopted the new faith. Egyptian Christians actually developed a different theology than that of other sects of the religion: They subscribed to the creed of mono-physitism, the belief that Jesus Christ was *not* both human and divine (as most Christians believe), but only divine in nature. Such Christians were called Copts, from the Greek work *Aiguptioi*, which means "Egyptian," and they made up a large segment of the Egyptian population at the time of the Islamic invasion.

In 632, the Muslim armies conquered the Romans (and the powerful Persian Byzantine empire) and threw them out of the lands of Syria, Palestine, and Egypt. Seven years later, they established complete domination over Egypt and began to spread Arabic language and culture to the newly conquered Egyptians. The Copts, who spoke a native Egyptian language called Demotic but used a Greek alphabet, began to speak, read, and write in Arabic, the language of their conquerors.

In many ways, however, the Muslims were tolerant of the native customs and culture of their new subjects. In the Koran, the holy book of Islam, Christians and Jews are referred to as "People of the Book." Muslims see Islam as an outgrowth and continuation of Christianity and Judaism, and they view people like Moses and Jesus as prophets. Many of the stories in the Bible are recounted in the Koran. Therefore, in general, the Muslims did not force the Egyptians to convert to Islam, but over time, many Copts did. Many Jews, who also made up a small segment of the Egyptian population, converted as well, but those Egyptians who did not surrender their Christian or Jewish faith did not suffer any penalties.

In fact, historian Glenn Perry noted in *The History of Egypt* that under the powerful Fatimid Muslim dynasty, which ruled between A.D. 909 and 1171, Jews enjoyed a "golden age" of political, religious, and cultural freedom. Likewise, many Copts also held high political and social positions and were accepted by the new Muslim rulers.

The era of Muslim rule in Egypt was a progressive time in the nation's history. For example, the Fatimids were Shiites, one of the two major sects of Islam (the other being the Sunni sect). It was the Fatimids who founded the city of Cairo and established it as the region's new capital. The city's name derives from the Arabic word *al-Qahira*, which means "the victorious," to commemorate their military success in Egypt. The Fatimids also patronized the arts and helped build a strong cultural life in Egypt.

Various Muslim dynasties vied for control of Egypt over the centuries. In 1174, Saladin, the great Muslim warrior who defeated the European Crusaders, made Egypt a Sunni Muslim country, and it has remained Sunni ever since. The Ottomans, who originated in Turkey (and thus were Muslims but not Arabs), conquered Egypt and most of the Middle East in 1516. Historians credit Mehmet Ali ("Mehmet" is the Turkish translation of the Arabic name Muhammad), an Ottoman pasha who ruled from 1805 to 1848, with modernizing Egypt. He promoted industry and education, and he strengthened the army. Arthur Goldschmidt, Jr., author of *Modern Egypt: The Formation of a Nation State,* wrote, "Mehmet Ali made Egypt a military power second to none in the Middle East."

Perhaps Ali felt compelled to solidify his military because of what had happened earlier, in 1798. In the summer of that year, Napoleon Bonaparte, the French general who would later become an emperor, invaded Egypt. The Ottomans had been compelled to seek help from the British, who were bitter enemies of the French at the time. An alliance between the two succeeded in driving the French out of Egypt in 1801. British soldiers remained stationed in Egypt, though, even after the threat of a war with France was over.

Mehmet Ali held reign from 1805 to 1848 and is considered to be the founder of modern Egypt. As an Ottoman pasha, Ali strengthened the Egyptian army, improved education, and promoted industrialization and agriculture.

The British reluctance to leave was not surprising. In fact, it was clear that the European powers recognized the strategic importance of Egypt and the benefits that could be gained by possessing it. Some Ottoman rulers often flirted with the idea of "Westernizing" Egypt and making its leaders more compliant to the wishes of Western leaders. After all, the British and the French had a lot of money that could be invested in Egypt. Pasha Said, the son of Mehmet Ali, supported the establishment of the Suez Canal Company, headed by French businessman Count Ferdinand de Lesseps. The project entailed building a canal that would allow ships to reach Asia without the burden and added time of having to sail around the African continent. The British realized the value of the canal, which would provide easier access to India, England's most prized colony. However, the French owned most of the canal, while the Egyptian government owned 44 percent of the shares.

The Suez Canal officially opened in 1869. However, Pasha Ismail, who succeeded Pasha Said, sold his government shares in 1875 because he had mismanaged the nation's funds and faced bankruptcy. The canal, a valuable Egyptian asset, was now completely owned by the British and French and out of Egyptian control. Ismail had brought Egypt even closer to European dominion. In 1878, he famously said, "My country is no longer in Africa; we are now a part of Europe." He could not have known it would take nearly another 75 years for Egypt to shake off Europe's influence.

3

Under Colonial Rule

IN 1882, THE BRITISH SUPPRESSED A POPULAR REVOLUTION WITHIN EGYPT.
Known as the Urabi Revolution, it began in 1881 when
Egyptians, led by Colonel Ahmad Urabi, protested the increasing level of influence the British government held over their
leaders. The British sought to protect their investment in the
Suez Canal, and they used the suppression of the revolution as
a way to formally occupy Egypt. Thus, in 1882, Egypt became
the latest addition to the British colonial empire. Sir Evelyn
Baring, known as Lord Cromer, became the representative of
the British government in Egypt, and he effectively ruled the
country for 24 years, beginning in 1883. Although he did not
enjoy a popular tenure with the Egyptian people, he did suc-
cessfully manage the massive debts and financial instability that
had been caused by Egypt's long line of fiscally irresponsible
pashas. Egyptians were unhappy with foreign rule, but the
financial situation improved for many people, even though the

The Suez Canal *(above)*, an important waterway connecting Europe and Asia, officially opened for traffic in 1869. Although there has been much conflict over ownership of the canal, Egyptian president Gamal Abdel Nasser nationalized the Suez Canal while he was in office.

positive changes rarely trickled down far enough to reach the poorest of society.

During this relatively stable era of British rule in Egypt's history, Arabs from around the region flocked to Egypt to work. Egypt, and especially Cairo, became a hub of culture, art, and literature for the Arab-speaking world. *Al-Ahram*, Egypt's most wellknown newspaper, for example, was established in 1875 by two Christian brothers who had emigrated from Lebanon. Book publishers and presses also flourished.

The arts flourished during this time period, as did a burgeoning anticolonial and independence movement. Most Egyptians resented being under British imperial rule and wanted an independent nation, free of Western influence. The resistance to the British occupation took two distinct paths: a pan-Islamic front and a secular nationalist movement. The first movement, the pan-Islamic movement, grew out of a desire of many to return to Islamic law and link Egypt as an Islamic nation to other Muslims in the Middle East and around the world. The second movement was secular and prioritized the Egyptian identity over the Muslim one and sought to include all the people of Egypt—Copts, Jews, and Muslims—in the effort to become an independent nation.

Both strands of the independence movement had much fuel to fire their motivation and desire for an independent Egypt. In 1906, for example, an incident occurred at Dinshaway, a small village near the Nile Delta. Five British soldiers wanted some recreation and decided to go pigeon shooting near the village. One of them accidentally shot at a grain pile and set it ablaze. The owner rushed at the soldier and attempted to take away his gun, and soon a brawl broke out. Five villagers were badly hurt, including the wife of the owner. Chaos erupted at the news, and the villagers attacked the soldiers, badly injuring two of them (one of the wounded British soldiers later died of heat stroke).

The British government considered the Dinshaway incident an attack on its nationals and decided to punish the villagers themselves, without involving the Egyptian government. Fifty-two villagers were arrested and accused of premeditated murder; the trials, held by a special tribunal, were heavily biased, and in the end, thirty-two of them were found guilty. While most of those found guilty were punished in varying ways, including floggings, four Egyptian villagers were executed by hanging.

Egyptians were outraged and felt that the British sentences had been excessively harsh. The incident became an opportunity for lower-class Egyptians to join forces with the middle-class intellectuals in calling for an end to British rule in their country. The uproar eventually caused so much controversy that Lord Cromer resigned from his position in 1907. Meanwhile, the pan-Islamic and the secular independence movements continued to increase in their fervor and to garner more popular support.

During World War I, the British hold over Egypt became even more obvious and pronounced. The Ottomans sided with Germany, England's enemy, during the war, prompting England to sever its ties with the Ottomans and declare a protectorate over Egypt. A "protectorate" essentially meant that Egypt would be governed, directly or indirectly, by a more powerful authority, England.

Egyptian nationalists had had enough. Life under the British had meant financial and economic stability for the nation, but the lower classes suffered from extreme poverty while the British citizens who lived in Egypt enjoyed a very posh lifestyle. The discrepancy had only become more and more pronounced over the years. The level of discrimination was also outstanding. For example, as John Solecki wrote in *Husni Mubarak,*

> British citizens living in Egypt during this time did not have to obey Egyptian law: if they committed any crimes or misdemeanors, they were tried in a special court for foreigners. This arrangement was a constant source of humiliation and anger for Egyptian nationalists.

Egyptians resented the fact that they were second-class citizens in their own country.

Such popular sentiments ushered in the era known as the 1919 Revolution. The key figure at its helm was Sa'ad Zaghlul, commonly referred to as "the father of the Egyptians." After World War I, when the Ottomans had been defeated and the British were in control, Zaghlul wanted to lead a delegation (or *wafd*, in Arabic) to London to request independence for Egypt. His request was denied, but it sparked the establishment of the Wafd Party, which became the loudest voice calling for a free and independent nation. In 1919, the British government exiled Zaghlul, but his exile only exacerbated the problem for the colonial forces, who had to deal with the anger of his many supporters.

Students take to the streets in Cairo, Egypt, in December 1919 to protest British occupancy. The 1919 Revolution, as it was called, was a nationalist movement in Egypt declaring independence from European rule. In February 1922, Egypt became an independent nation.

The 1919 Revolution was essentially a secular independence movement that included men and women of all segments of the Egyptian population: Copts, Muslims, and Jews all contributed their efforts to the movement. Demonstrations were held regularly, and a massive boycott of British goods was organized. Their efforts were rewarded in 1922. Unable to sustain the political and social pressure of the revolution, the British signed an agreement ending their protectorate over Egypt. Essentially, Egypt was now free to govern its own affairs, except for "Four Points" outlined in the agreement. The points were that, despite Egypt's new independence, England would retain control over its communications within Egypt; it reserved the right to defend Egypt against foreign attack; it possessed authority over British citizens living within Egypt; and it continued its rule over Sudan, Egypt's southern neighbor. Thus, England still controlled issues that were central to Egypt, including control over some members of the population, communications, and military defense. The end to the British protectorate over Egypt was obviously not full independence, but it was a significant step in that direction.

The agreement also resulted in the establishment of a monarchy in Egypt. Sultan Ahmed Fuad became King Fuad and Egypt's new leader. In 1923, a constitution was drafted and approved, establishing a democratic system that was—as it soon became apparent—anything but democratic. The king was the final authority on all social and political matters, and political parties, such as the Wafd Party, had little influence in government; furthermore, the British continued to exercise their powerful influence over Egyptian affairs through King Fuad, who was generally obliging and acquiesced to their demands.

King Fuad and his son, King Faruq, who succeeded him in 1936, essentially dismissed the 1923 constitution and ignored the requirements that it set forth. The Egyptian monarchy felt that its power was threatened by the Wafd Party, which controlled most of the seats in the Parliament and which consistently, and loudly, called for democratic reform. Because the British government supported the king against the Wafd, the people considered the king to be corrupt and a mere puppet of the British, who still wanted to retain their colonial influence.

The 1936 Anglo-Egyptian Treaty of Alliance reduced the British presence in the country even further, establishing an alliance between the two countries for 20 years. For example, one tenet of the treaty stated that England would maintain the presence of its troops in the Suez Canal until 1956. However, troops in other areas of the country were removed.

In that same year, however, Egypt's financial situation became more dire. The price of cotton—one of the country's main exports—fell to a precipitous level. Mass poverty crippled the countryside and scores of people flocked to Cairo,

The photograph above shows the opening of the Egyptian Parliament in 1926. King Fuad, the first king of Egypt, sits on the throne while members of the royal house are seated to the left, and the new cabinet is seated on the right.

desperate for work. In fact, Cairo's population, which had been less than 800,000 in 1917, swelled to more than 2 million by the late 1940s. Dissatisfaction with the government continued to grow. People briefly had hope for change when King Faruq succeeded his father, but as historian Arthur Goldschmidt, Jr., wrote in *Modern Egypt*, that hope faded when people realized that "Faruq turned out to be as dictatorial as his father had been."

The Wafd Party, which had enjoyed favor as the voice of opposition, fell into a crisis. Its reputation slowly diminished as people looked elsewhere for a strong representative to combat the king's corruption. The Islamic independence movement steadily gained public favor during this time, especially as the secular nationalist movement's influence waned along with that of the Wafd Party. The pro-Islamic movement was led by the Society of Muslim Brothers.

The Society of Muslim Brothers had been founded in 1928 by Hasan al-Banna with the intent of establishing an Islamic government in Egypt. Its leaders rejected secularism as fervently as they rejected the British colonial influence. They believed that a return to Islamic law would restore the nation's power, currently languishing under foreign control. The society gained support among the people by establishing a pseudo-welfare system during the difficult years of the 1930s.

The Society of Muslim Brothers also latched onto another cause, besides the domestic issue of poverty—the regional dilemma that was brewing in neighboring Palestine. After the British ousted the Ottomans from Palestine after World War I, Palestinian Arabs expected the independence that the British had promised. However, the British had also promised European Jews that they could establish a Jewish homeland in the same area. By the early 1900s, Jews from Europe began emigrating to Palestine in large numbers. By 1936, open hostility existed between the Jewish émigrés and the native Palestinian population, and though both looked to the colonial British power for a resolution, none seemed forthcoming. Thus, both communities turned their anger and frustration upon the British as well. In 1936, the native Palestinians staged a revolt against both the British and the Jewish, or Zionist, populations. The revolt garnered the support of many neighboring Arab countries. Arthur Goldschmidt, Jr., wrote, "Newly independent Iraq and Egypt tried to help them politically and economically more than militarily." Of course, it would have been impossible for Egypt, still under British influence, to lend military support to an anti-British revolt.

The Egyptian people generally supported the Palestinians, with a few of them—namely the pan-Islamists—seeing the

Founded in Egypt in 1928 by Hassan al-Banna and six members of the Suez Canal Company, the Society of Muslim Brothers, also known as the "Brotherhood," is a worldwide fundamentalist Islamic movement. The organization's emblem is shown above.

struggle as part of a larger Muslim resistance against Western-imposed colonialism. Other Egyptians also gave their support but maintained an "Egypt-first" mentality that some have called "pharaonism," or a belief that being Egyptian was an ethnic identity distinct from the Arab identity. Thus, Egyptian domestic concerns were more pressing than those of other Arabs in the region.

By 1936, in fact, three forms of nationalism had developed in Egypt, all opposed to British influence but in different ways. One was the pan-Islamist movement, mentioned before and largely represented by the Society of Muslim Brothers. A second was the pharaonism movement, which was dedicated to

Egyptian nationalism and independence but did not view the Egyptian identity as connected to the Arab one. The third was a pan-Arab nationalist movement, which connected Egyptian independence to the nationalist movements occurring in other Arab nations in the region, such as the one in Palestine. However, as the crisis in Palestine intensified, the majority of the Egyptian people began to associate themselves with the other Arabs in the region and to develop a sense of loyalty to Arab causes in general.

After World War II and the horror of the Holocaust in Europe, in which millions of Jews were systematically killed by the German Nazi regime, world-wide sympathy for the plight of the Jews increased. As a result, the call for an independent Jewish state grew louder. The rate of Jewish immigration to Palestine increased rapidly.

In 1947, the British decided to turn the issue of who had a right to Palestine over to the United Nations to solve. The result was a decision to partition Palestine into a Jewish state and a Palestinian state, with the hotly contested city of Jerusalem becoming an internationalized zone. Because a majority of the land (55 percent) was allotted to the minority Jewish population (they composed only 33 percent of the population of Palestine at the time), the Palestinians rejected the partition plan. In 1948, however, when England formally ended its mandate over Palestine, the Jews declared the establishment of the state of Israel.

The neighboring Arab countries, including Egypt, Jordan, Syria, and Lebanon, declared war on Israel but were defeated. The loss was devastating to the Arab nations, and it changed the landscape of politics in Egypt forever. Israel became Egypt's main enemy and the defeat led to the increase in the popularity of the Society of Muslim Brothers and a resounding fury and unhappiness with King Faruq and the British. Israel's defeat of the Arabs in 1948 ensured that things in the region would never be the same.

4

Independence
at Last

DURING THE POLITICAL TURMOIL OF THE 1920S AND 1930S, EGYPT WAS
undergoing major changes, dealing with a new monarchal government, resisting the British forces, and reacting to a growing sense
of nationalism that was largely pan-Arabist. In 1929, in the midst
of this turbulent time, a future leader was born who would, at the
very least, bring stability.

On May 4, 1929, Muhammad Hosni Mubarak was born in
Kafr-al-Meselha, in the Nile Delta region in northern Egypt. His
family lived a humble lifestyle and was not rich. Like many young
men of his generation, Mubarak decided that the best route to
a successful career was through the military. In November 1947,
when he was 18 years old, he enrolled in the Egyptian Military
Academy. He graduated fewer than two years later and entered
the Egyptian Air Academy, where he became an air force pilot.

In March 1952, Mubarak graduated from the Air Academy.
"As a pilot," wrote John Solecki in his biography of Mubarak,

"he was among the best at flying the British Spitfire fighters." He was respected for his talents in the air force, and this would serve him well politically, especially because 1952 was the year when everything would change in Egypt.

Since the 1948 defeat of the Egyptian army (and of other Arab militaries) at the hands of the nascent Israeli state, there had been a revolution quietly brewing within the ranks of Egypt's military. Its leader was an intelligent, earnest, and charismatic young officer named Gamal Abdel Nasser.

Nasser was born in 1918 in the village of Bacos, a small suburb of Alexandria in northern Egypt. His family was originally from the poor village of Beni Morr near Asyut in southern Egypt. Like the families of many of the people who would later serve with him in the military, Nasser's family came from a humble financial background. His father was a post office clerk, his mother a homemaker. The family had 11 children, of which he was the eldest.

As a child, Gamal Abdel Nasser spent much time with an uncle who lived in Cairo. His uncle held anti-colonialist views, and young Gamal himself joined anti-British demonstrations as a schoolboy. He did not do well in school, failing several times. He enlisted in the military and served with honor during the 1948 Arab-Israeli War. Like many men in his situation, the military offered an opportunity for a career and a stable, if not lavish, lifestyle.

Perhaps it was the 1948 war, however, that shaped Nasser's political agenda and vision for the future of Egypt. As he bravely fought in battle, even sustaining an injury from a sniper's bullet in his shoulder, he came to realize that there was massive corruption within the military's highest ranks. The corruption could be traced as high up the chain of command as King Faruq himself. The distance between the commanders and the soldiers on the field was astonishingly wide, making communication difficult. Fighting conditions were also poor; soldiers were often left to fight with outdated weapons. "Often the soldiers' guns misfired and their grenades sometimes exploded in their hands," wrote Solecki in *Husni Mubarak*. Even worse, the money intended for the purchase of more modern equipment was being used to pad the coffers of the corrupt King Faruq and his friends. Nasser was disgusted with the behavior of the government and saw the situation as indicative of an impending decline of Egypt, unless action was taken to remedy the problem.

Indeed, Egypt had suffered from many problems in the mid-1940s and early 1950s. King Faruq was viewed as not only a corrupt puppet of the Western powers, but also as a gambler and womanizer whose behavior embarrassed his people, most of whom lived a modest, conservative lifestyle. Furthermore, the Wafd Party, which had been seen as the voice of nationalism and independence in the past, was also riddled with corruption at its highest levels and seen as lacking credibility.

In addition, the continuing rise of the Society of Muslim Brothers became a real cause for concern. Determined to overthrow the current government and to establish one based on Islamic law, some members of the brotherhood turned to violence. They formed a wing known as al-Jihaz al-Sirri, or the "Secret Apparatus," which carried out assassinations and other terrorist acts. In December 1948, after the Arab-Israeli War, the Secret Apparatus murdered Prime Minister Mahmoud Fahmi Nuqrashi for his attempts to outlaw the Society of Muslim Brothers. The following year, in an act largely believed to have been ordered by King Faruq, the founder of the brotherhood, Hassan al-Banna, was himself assassinated.

The ascent of real revolt—and the increase in violence—were proof of the climbing level of frustration of the people with the rule of King Faruq and his government. This frustration stirred Nasser to assemble colleagues in the military, among the ranks of other officers, to mount a revolution. Calling themselves the Free Officers, they included men like Anwar Sadat and Muhammad Najib. Together, under Nasser's primary influence and guidance, they planned a coup,

In 1936, Prince Farouk succeeded his father as the king of Egypt. Farouk was known as much for his lavish lifestyle as his corrupt government. In 1952, he was exiled to Italy and his title was given to his son, Fuad II. Above, King Farouk is photographed in his formal uniform, circa 1940.

intending to stage it within the next few years. The opportunity, however, arrived sooner than they had intended because of an event known as Black Saturday.

In January of 1952, England accused Egyptian police officers of supporting attacks on the British troops who were stationed near the Suez Canal region. The British attacked the Egyptian police force, killing 50 men, an act that infuriated the Egyptian people, who correctly interpreted the event as yet another symbol of how the country was not really free of imperial rule and interference. On January 26, Egyptians revolted in the streets of Cairo, setting fires and sparking chaos. In an effort to calm the situation, King Faruq imposed strict martial law, which, not surprisingly, only aggravated the frustrations of the people. "Black Saturday was the collective expression of many Egyptians' hostility to Western wealth, power, and cultural influence," wrote Goldschmidt in *Modern Egypt*. The outrageousness of Black Saturday—and King Faruq's response—prompted the Free Officers to act sooner than expected.

On July 23, 1952, the Free Officers put their plan into action—and succeeded. In a calm and bloodless coup d'etat, 300 officers seized control of the government. They ousted King Faruq and escorted him on July 26 to a ship that sailed to the Italian Riviera, exiling him permanently from the country.

The Free Officers agreed to allow the king's young son to rule as regent, but, a year later, in June 1953, the group disposed of the system of monarchy altogether and declared Egypt a free republic. General Muhammad Najib, rather than Nasser, the group's actual leader, was named the new Egyptian president. Many claim that it was Nasser's own idea to install Najib, the eldest of the Free Officers, at the helm of the new government, while Nasser exerted his influence from a less prominent position. Over the next year, however, a power struggle ensued between the two men. In April of 1954, Nasser ousted Najib and assumed the leadership role himself.

UNDER NASSER, THESE CORE VALUES OF THE FREE OFFICERS REMAINED IN PLACE, AND THEY WON THE GROUP THE RESPECT OF THE EGYPTIAN PEOPLE.

The Free Officers were a diverse group. They held varying political ties and affiliations. Anwar Sadat, for example, was known to be sympathetic to the Society of Muslim Brothers, while Nasser was a secularist. However, the Free Officers agreed unanimously on the importance of social justice, a strong military, and government by parliamentary rule. They also adamantly rejected imperial interference and capitalism. The dignity of a sovereign Egypt had to be maintained by not allowing Western or other foreign powers to wield their influence.

Under Nasser, these core values of the Free Officers remained in place, and they won the group the respect of the Egyptian people. For example, the Free Officers issued a land-reform policy that redistributed land from the feudal landlords to the peasants and farmers who worked on it. The policy was immensely popular and won massive support for the new government.

Not all Egyptians were happy with Nasser. In October 1954, the Society of Muslim Brothers attempted to assassinate him because he advocated a secular, pan-Arab nationalist movement. In response, Nasser cracked down on the organization, executing six of its members and imprisoning thousands more.

Many people outside of Egypt also disliked Nasser, who quickly made enemies among the Western governments, especially England and France, when he nationalized the Suez Canal in 1956. The British had pulled their troops out of the Canal Zone in June 1956, according to the 1936 Anglo-Egyptian Treaty, but they, along with the French, still owned the canal (due to Pasha Ismail's selling of the Egyptian government's

In the photograph above, a tank parks outside the National Bank of Egypt in Cairo, following the coup that forced the abdication of King Farouk. The tank was a precautionary measure taken by Major General Mohammed Naguid. King Farouk was forced into exile with his wife, Queen Marriman, and their infant son and future king, Prince Ahmed Fuad.

shares in the corporation). In July 1956, Nasser proclaimed during a speech: "In the name of the Government of Egypt, I inform you that the Suez Canal Company is nationalized and I have come to take over the premises." At that moment, Egyptian soldiers entered the offices of de Lesseps and seized control.

Nasser's bold move resulted from his anger at the United States, which had agreed to support Nasser's project to build a dam at Aswan. However, at the last moment, the United States backed out of its promise, which embarrassed and infuriated the Egyptian president, who had been touting the endeavor. Nationalizing the Suez Canal would generate immense profits for the Egyptian government and support the building of the Aswan High Dam. In addition, Nasser generally viewed the British and French ownership of the Suez Canal as a last remnant of colonialism; by nationalizing his country's biggest asset, he eradicated the last traces of imperial influence in his country.

The British and French governments were furious about Nasser's nationalization of the canal. In October 1956, along with Israel, they coordinated an attack on Egypt. They invaded the country and, as the Egyptian forces were no match for them, they encountered little resistance. By early November, they had seized control of the canal. Internationally, the British, French, and Israeli attack was widely condemned, especially by countries like India (which had itself only won independence from British colonialism in 1947).

The international response was the only thing that saved Egypt and Nasser's government. The three invading powers were pressured to withdraw, which they did by early 1957, and the Suez Canal eventually reverted to full Egyptian control.

Though the Egyptians had technically suffered an invasion of their country, the final victory belonged to Nasser. He became a hero to the Egyptian people and to Arabs all over the Middle East for withstanding (and effectively winning) a battle against three major foreign powers. He was seen as a leader who put the needs of the people first and who stood up to the Western powers. With his new stature as a hero secured, Nasser pushed for his dream of Arab unity by encouraging the formation of the Arab League in 1945, with its headquarters in Cairo.

In 1956, a new constitution cemented Nasser's power. It established a strong, central presidency, supported by a consultative assembly. All political parties, except for the National Union Party, were banned so that it was virtually impossible to challenge Nasser's power and rule. Nasser believed capitalism

Gamal Abdel Nasser, the president of Egypt from 1956 to 1970 is photographed during his first year in office. While in office, Nasser nationalized the Suez Canal. Revered as one of the greatest Arab leaders, the nation of Egypt mourned his death when he died of a heart attack in 1970. He was succeeded by Anwar Sadat.

only led to major discrepancies in class and to the exploitation of the poorer segments of society. He advocated Socialism instead, in which the government owns the major means of production and guarantees economic stability for all people. Nasser instituted his policy of Arab Socialism through a series of laws passed in 1961, which came to be known as the July Socialist Laws. Some of these included the nationalization of most of the financial sector and of foreign imports, as well as rules placing limits on the number of shares individuals could hold in Egyptian companies.

Socialist Nasser was not a Communist, but he did begin to draw closer to the Soviet Union. He believed his country should not take sides in the Cold War brewing between the

United States and the USSR, but he remembered how the United States had reneged on its promise of help with the Aswan High Dam project. The Soviets proved to be more trustworthy allies, and they supplied Nasser with modern equipment and weapons, such as tanks and planes. They also invited Egyptian military officers to train at Soviet military academies. The Soviet help was invaluable, as one of Nasser's main priorities was to enhance the Egyptian military. The British, French, and Israeli attack in 1956 had taught him a lesson about allowing the country to be vulnerable.

At this time, Hosni Mubarak was an instructor for other pilots in the Air Academy. As he built a career for himself, his personal life was also changing rapidly. In the late 1950s, he met the sister of one of his academy students.

Suzanne Sabet was born in 1941 in Menya, a city located along the Nile River. Her father was an Egyptian doctor and her mother was a nurse from Wales. Sabet studied at an all-girls school in Heliopolis and did very well academically. She spoke Arabic and English fluently. She and Mubarak were married in 1958. After their marriage, Sabet, now Suzanne Mubarak, continued her studies.

Mubarak's star continued to rise. Anwar Sadat attended an airfield training exercise and took note of Mubarak's intelligence and cleverness. In February 1964, he was selected to attend the Frunze Military Academy in the Soviet province in central Asia. During his studies of more than a year, he also learned to speak Russian. Like Nasser, he appreciated the benefits of an informal alliance with the Soviet Union, but he was not won over by Communist ideology.

5

A Major Defeat and the Era of Sadat

IN 1967, ARAB-ISRAELI TENSIONS WERE STEADILY WORSENING. BY THE spring, another war was inevitable. Egypt and Syria amassed their troops on the Israeli border, but Israel attacked first on June 5, in a surprise air strike that devastated the Arab air forces. In a few hours, the Egyptian, Syrian, Jordanian, and Iraqi airplanes, which were still on the ground, were destroyed. The Arab forces never recovered from this initial blow, and Israel soon captured the Sinai Peninsula; the Palestinian territories of the Gaza Strip, East Jerusalem, and the West Bank of the Jordan River; and the Syrian territory of the Golan Heights. By the time a cease-fire was declared six days later, the Arab world was stunned by its immense loss. Not only had they been defeated yet again by the Israelis, but the Arabs lost more land rather than regained it.

An Israeli soldier lines up captured Egyptian troops during the 1967 Six-Day War. The war resulted in Israel acquiring the Gaza Strip, the Sinai Peninsula, the West Bank, and Golan Heights. Current political conflict in the area can be attributed to the Israeli success in the Six-Day War.

Nasser suffered especially from this defeat, which seemed to undermine his emphasis on Arab unity and Arab power. He resigned from the presidency, but a popular demonstration on the streets of Egypt made him change his mind; the Egyptian people wanted his continued leadership despite the defeat, demonstrating Nasser's immense popularity. The defeat in the 1967 war prompted him to make several changes in the government and military, including firing many officers who were blamed for the military's poor performance in battle. According to John Solecki in his biography of Mubarak, "This was a very important step for Egypt, and for Mubarak, because it cleared the way for younger officers to move up in rank."

Indeed, Mubarak moved up the ranks very quickly. In November 1967, the popular instructor was appointed director general of the Air Academy. In June of 1969, he received yet another promotion to chief of staff of the air force. Later that year, Nasser chose as vice president Anwar Sadat, who had taken notice of Hosni Mubarak's intelligence and abilities and respected the young officer. This connection would eventually prove fruitful for Mubarak's political career.

On September 28, 1970, Nasser died of a sudden heart attack. The Arab world and especially Egypt was shaken by the death of a political giant, a leader who had done so much to modernize and stabilize Egypt. Millions of people attended his funeral, making it the largest funeral ever at that point in time. People throughout many Arab nations genuinely mourned his loss. The leaders of Western nations, though, were not so grieved because of their many political differences with Nasser.

The grief over Nasser's death in Egypt was overwhelming. Anwar Sadat, who would replace him as the new president, even fainted at the funeral. However, although he had been loyal to Nasser, Sadat was a very different leader than his predecessor. He wanted to court the Western powers, such as the United States, in order to help boost Egypt's sagging economy. Nasser's Arab socialism program had encouraged young Egyptians, especially those from the lower classes, to improve their circumstances through higher education, but these college graduates often could not find employment except in the swelling, low-paying civil servant job positions.

Sadat launched a program called *al-infitah*, or "the opening," in which he opened the doors of the Egyptian economy to capitalist interests. This was a major shift from Nasser's Arab socialist program. As Arthur Goldschmidt, Jr., wrote in *Modern Egypt*, "Although Sadat still paid lip service to Arab nationalism, he moved toward an Egypt-first policy" that sought to benefit from better relationships with wealthier Western nations. Courting the West and making it easier for its businesses to invest in Egypt meant that Sadat also had to distance himself and Egypt from the Soviet Union. The Cold War and tensions between the United States and the Soviet Union were still intense, and Sadat didn't want to risk Egypt's relationship with the United States. He actually took the bold step of expelling the Soviets from Egypt in July 1972. When one of his military advisors protested the move, Sadat replaced him with Hosni Mubarak. Mubarak now commanded the Egyptian Air Force and was named the deputy minister of war in Sadat's cabinet.

At first, Sadat's policies were generally well-received by the people of Egypt. Sadat became even more popular when he launched the 1973 Yom Kippur War against Israel. Coordinated with Syria during top-secret meetings, the attack surprised everyone. The plan was for Egyptian forces to attack the Israelis in the Sinai, which was still occupied by Israel, while the Syrians would attack in the Israeli-occupied Golan Heights from the north. Yom Kippur, the Jewish holy day of atonement and an important religious holiday, was chosen because it was expected that the Israelis would be caught off guard.

Indeed they were. When the attack was launched on October 6, 1973, the Arab forces acted swiftly and efficiently. Mubarak especially delivered several victories for Egypt. As John Solecki explained in *Husni Mubarak*, "Under Mubarak's direction, the Egyptian air force performed well, carrying out effective air strikes against Israeli targets in the Sinai." After several days of fighting, the Israelis recouped their strength and fought back, leading to a deadlock. The United Nations brokered a cease-fire, to which all sides agreed on October 24. Although the war was not technically a victory for Egypt, neither was it a military win for Israel. In that sense, Egypt viewed it as the first Arab-Israeli war in which its forces had performed well and did significant damage to the Israeli military. The military leaders who had fought in the war became known as the October Generation. Mubarak especially garnered high praise for his command of the air force and his role in helping to prepare the Egyptian offensive. On February 19, 1974, he earned yet another promotion, to air marshal of the Egyptian Air Force.

Anwar Sadat's popularity among his people reached a peak, a real coup considering the immense and overwhelming popularity of his predecessor, Gamal Abdel Nasser. However, Sadat quickly squandered any goodwill among his people that he may have earned as a result of the 1973 war. Part of this was caused by his continued courting of the Western powers, especially the United States. Many Arabs disliked the American government because it had supported Israel militarily during the 1973 war and previous wars. As Mark Tessler is quoted in John Solecki's book, "Many in Egypt saw Sadat's failure as at least partly the result of the government's close relationship with the United States." Sadat had many reasons, besides economic ones, for building a friendship: He knew the United States was influential with the Israelis and could be used to negotiate an Israeli withdrawal from the Egyptian Sinai Peninsula. He was once quoted as saying frankly that "America has 99 percent of the cards."

He made it clear to the United States that, if it became involved, he would be willing to enter negotiations with the Israelis to work out a post-war agreement as well as a larger peace initiative between the two nations. U.S. secretary of state Henry Kissinger helped work out an agreement that called upon the Israelis to disengage their forces from the Suez Canal's east bank, to be replaced by a United Nations peacekeeping force. This agreement was signed by both parties on January 17, 1974. Egyptians were stunned that Sadat had

Anwar Sadat is photographed with U.S. president Gerald Ford at a banquet in Salzburg, Austria, in 1975. Unlike his predecessor Gamal Abdel Nasser, Sadat wanted to strengthen ties with the West while he was in office. Although his popularity with the Egyptian population started to decline, Sadat strengthened Egypt's relationship with the United States.

entered into an agreement with Israel without consulting or involving other Arab nations. Soon, as further Egyptian-Israeli negotiations ensued, Sadat became deeply unpopular, viewed as a "yes-man" to the United States.

On the domestic front, his al-infitah policy was also losing support. Since Nasser's time, the Egyptian government had subsidized the prices of many necessary goods, such as bread. Sadat, however, decided on an economic policy to reduce those subsidies, which led to a sharp rise in the cost of everyday necessities. The price of bread, for example, practically doubled. Panicked and outraged, Egyptians rioted in January 1977, protesting al-infitah. The riots, known as the Bread Riots, led to the deaths of approximately 150 people.

Sadat also continued to eliminate any elements of Nasserism from his government. He renamed the Arab Socialist Union, which had been Nasser's party, the National Democratic Party (NDP). He fired people from his government who had been part of Nasser's coterie or who had shown loyalty to Nasser's ideals. In April 1975, Vice President Hussein Shafei was fired and replaced with the military's rising star, Hosni Mubarak.

Mubarak had never held a governmental position before, and his naturally quiet style led to a popular assumption that he had been chosen by Sadat because he was agreeable and would not cause debate. Some believe, however, that his public demeanor belied how active he actually was behind the scenes. Nevertheless, in Egyptian circles, Mubarak earned the unfortunate nickname of "La Vache Qui Rit," or "Laughing Cow," because of an alleged physical resemblance to the logo of a popular French cheese spread by the same name sold in the Middle East.

The Egyptians' general dislike of Mubarak was most likely linked to their dislike of Anwar Sadat, whose reputation was sinking quickly. Although he had begun his presidency by seeming to vanquish corruption in the government, his own leadership was becoming corrupt itself. Al-infitah had led to a decreased economic status for most Egyptians, while a few elite citizens became wealthy. It was not a coincidence that many of these people were close associates and relatives of the president.

Sadat's greatest flaw in the eyes of his people remained his close association with the West, which was reflected in his lifestyle. He and his wife, Jehan Sadat, lived extravagantly, owning glamorous homes, throwing costly parties, and dressing in the latest Western fashions. He also allegedly arranged for family and friends to receive lucrative government contracts and positions with high salaries. In contrast, during his own presidency, Gamal Abdel Nasser had maintained a humble lifestyle, allowing few frills for himself, his family, or his associates as a result of

On September 17, 1978, after 12 days of secret negotiations, Egyptian president Anwar Sadat *(left)*, U.S. president Jimmy Carter *(center)*, and Israeli prime minister Menachem Begin *(right)* make a bold move toward achieving peace in the Middle East as they sign one of two agreements of the Camp David Accords. Mediated by Carter, the peace agreements were the first between Israel and an Arab neighboring nation.

his position. In fact, a widely circulated anecdote claimed that Nasser's chauffeur's child passed the national examination to enter the university, while Nasser's own daughter failed it by only a few points, and the president refused to intervene to make an exception for her. Sadat, however, was different. Egyptians frequently pointed to the stark contrast between his own luxurious lifestyle and their meager ones.

The greatest criticism of Sadat was yet to come. In 1977, Sadat became determined to arrange a peace treaty between Egypt and Israel. Peace with Israel would mean a better—and more prosperous—relationship with the United States and a boon to Egypt's economy. On November 9, he told the Egyptian People's Assembly,

> I state in all seriousness that I am prepared to go to the end of the world—and Israel will be surprised to hear me tell you that I am ready to go to their home, to the Knesset itself, to argue with them, in order to prevent one Egyptian soldier from being wounded.

When Sadat made good on his promise later that month, however, the world was stunned. Sadat flew to Jerusalem and delivered a speech before the Knesset, the Israeli parliament, and argued that peace was necessary. The trip was praised as a bold move toward peace by the West, while Egypt and the rest of the Arab world viewed it as a betrayal, a recognition of Israel despite its continued occupation of Palestinian territories and other Arab lands.

On September 17, 1978, after almost two solid weeks of negotiations between Egypt and Israel—moderated by American president Jimmy Carter—Anwar Sadat and Israeli prime minister Menachem Begin signed the Camp David Accords. The historic ceremony took place at the White House and outlined a major settlement, the first by an Arab nation with its Israeli neighbor. The Sinai would be returned to Egypt in exchange for Egypt's recognition of Israel and an opening of a diplomatic and economic relationship between the two nations. The formal agreement was signed on March 26, 1979.

As Arthur Goldschmidt, Jr., wrote in *Modern Egypt*, "Egypt's peace treaty with Israel made it a ward of the West." Indeed, Egypt began receiving $2 billion annually in aid from the United States after the Camp David Accords went into effect. However, all Arab nations (except Somalia, Oman, and Sudan) broke off diplomatic ties with Egypt. It was further expelled from organizations such as the Arab League (which, ironically, Nasser had helped establish years earlier).

Egypt had made new friends, but it had isolated itself from almost all its former ones.

CHAPTER

6

The Islamic Revolution

IN 1979, THE PRO-WESTERN SHAH OF IRAN, MOHAMED REZA PAHLAVI, WAS overthrown by a revolutionary force headed by the right-wing cleric Ayatollah Khomeini. Soon, an era of Islamic conservatism swept into Iran, which became a country whose legal and political systems were dictated by Islamic law. In Egypt, the Society of Muslim Brothers and other Islamic groups viewed the Iranian revolution as a harbinger of what would eventually happen in their own country. Anwar Sadat angered many among the Islamic movement when he invited Iran's exiled Shah to seek asylum in Egypt. When the Shah, who was very ill, died, Sadat gave him a state funeral with many honors.

As membership in the Society of Muslim Brothers and other Islamic groups swelled, Anwar Sadat realized that he would have to address some of their concerns. To boost his popularity among them, he tried to tone down his extravagant lifestyle and appear more pious. He also began insisting on being addressed by his real first name, Muhammad.

His efforts essentially failed to win him more support. A phenomenon that could not be denied was sweeping through Egypt after the 1979 Iranian revolution—the rise of an ultra-conservative Islamic movement that made the members of the Society of Muslim Brothers no longer a political minority.

Many Islamic groups sprung up in Egypt. Not all of them were incorruptible. Sadat eventually learned how to forge uneasy alliances with the more radical groups. One of these, simply calling itself the Islamic Group, was a militant organization that advocated violence. Sadat used the Islamic Group and others like it to intimidate and silence his many critics, especially those among the intellectual segment of Egyptian society. He silenced those who called for a return to Nasser-era policies as well as those who were Communist sympathizers (especially since he was now an ally of the capitalist West).

In September 1981, Sadat ordered the arrests of more than 1,500 critics and political opponents. This action stunned Egyptians, and it portrayed Sadat as nothing more than a corrupt, paranoid dictator. The public frustration with Sadat's administration climaxed, paralleling the frustration people felt in the days of King Faruq.

On October 6, 1981, the government celebrated the anniversary of the 1973 Arab-Israeli War with a military parade. Sadat was standing up in his viewing box to salute passing soldiers when one of them, Khalid al-Islambuli, opened fire suddenly. Al-Islambuli's brother had been one of the people arrested a month earlier. As he killed Sadat, pelting him with bullets, al-Islambuli is said to have declared, "I have killed Pharaoh."

Seven other people who were in the viewing box with Sadat also died. Many more suffered injuries, including Vice President Hosni Mubarak. Later that same day, Mubarak announced Sadat's death to the nation and the world: "Choked with emotion," he said, "my tongue is unable to

Egyptian president Anwar Sadat was assassinated in October 1981. Members of an Islamic extremist organization took responsibility for the killing, claiming they did not agree with his peace negotiations with Israel. Vice President Hosni Mubarak *(center)* succeeded Anwar Sadat.

eulogize to the Egyptian nation, the Arab and Islamic people, and the whole world the struggling leader and hero, Anwar Sadat. . . . The leader to whom millions of hearts are attached is martyred."

Despite Mubarak's solemn words and grieving tone, the funeral of Sadat radically differed from that of his predecessor, Gamal Abdel Nasser. Millions of Egyptians had turned out, weeping and wailing, for Nasser's funeral, but there was little evidence of public grief for Sadat's death. The Egyptian people largely viewed him as a corrupt leader who had lived a lavish lifestyle, granting favors for friends and relatives who also became rich, while the majority of Egyptians struggled to make ends meet. Many observed that more people in the West grieved for the slain Arab leader than in the Middle East itself.

The mixed reaction to Sadat's death was not surprising. In the West, Sadat was hailed as a hero who bravely took on the challenge of making peace with Israel, an avant-garde leader with a broad vision. The Arab world generally felt that Sadat had betrayed them in signing a peace treaty with Israel that did not comprehensively address Arab and Palestinian grievances with the Jewish state. There was also a generally held view that Sadat had sold out to the United States at the expense of Egyptian and Arab concerns and needs.

After Sadat's assassination, skirmishes broke out between the Egyptian police and Islamic fundamentalists. Al-Islambuli and the three others who were implicated in the assassination belonged to a group known as Al-Jihad, and al-Islambuli publicly declared, "I am guilty of killing Sadat and I admit that. I am proud of it because the cause of religion was at stake." Indeed, many fundamentalists considered Sadat's death a first major step in attaining the goal of an Islamic government in Egypt. In Asyut, a small city south of Cairo, Egyptian police struggled for three days to suppress an uprising of fundamentalists; more than 50 police officers and many more insurgents were killed in the gun fight. Over the next several days following Sadat's killing, more than 2,500 people were accused of religious extremism and insurgent activities, and were arrested. The government eventually reimposed a set of Emergency Laws (originally declared in 1958) that allowed it widespread powers, and it enforced them harshly to maintain order.

On October 13, Hosni Mubarak was elected to succeed Anwar Sadat as the new president of Egypt. He was, in fact, the only candidate on the ballot. As Arthur Goldschmidt, Jr., wrote, Sadat "bequeathed to Mubarak a country at peace with Israel, but not with its Arab neighbors, and certainly not with itself." Hosni Mubarak's tasks—to restore order, fix the failing economy, and improve Egypt's status among its Arab neighbors while maintaining a solid relationship with the United States and continuing Egypt's progression and modernization—hardly were enviable ones. Furthermore, he did not want to earn the mixed legacy of his predecessor.

Mubarak began his presidency by distancing himself from Sadat's behavior and policies. For example, he ordered the release of the more than 1,500 people whom Sadat had had arrested in September 1981. Mubarak even met with them, perhaps to reassure them that they would not be targeted again. In a popular move, he also cracked down on corruption in the government, unveiling and eliminating many of Sadat's unethical policies. In fact, during his first speech to the nation, on November 1981, Mubarak promised the people "not to commit myself to what I cannot implement, hide the truth from the people, or be lenient with corruption and disorder."

One notable example was the corruption trial of Anwar Sadat's half brother, Esmat Sadat. A former bus driver, Esmat Sadat had become a millionaire during his brother's tenure in office. However, during a trial that captured the nation's attention, Esmat Sadat was found guilty of profiteering; his three sons were also found guilty, and all received a sentence of one year in jail and steep fines. Many other people who worked with Anwar Sadat and profited illegally were also exposed during Mubarak's crackdown on corruption. This group of people, a small group of wealthy businessmen known as the Mungatihun, were relentlessly targeted for illegally and unethically benefiting during Sadat's presidency.

Another criticism of Anwar Sadat had been the high public profile of his wife, Jehan Sadat, whose photo frequently appeared in the national and international press and who was seen at all the important social events in Cairo. She also had her own staff in the presidential palace. Many Egyptians felt that she led a glamorous lifestyle. It was ostentatious and offensive to the many Egyptians who languished in poverty.

Following Anwar Sadat's untimely death, Hosni Mubarak is sworn in as Egypt's new president. Mubarak rose to power in the Egyptian Air Force before becoming vice president to Anwar Sadat.

In contrast, Mubarak wanted to avoid the same controversy; already a low-profile person, Mubarak instructed the press to leave his family out of their papers, and neither to mention the names nor publish the photos of his wife, Suzanne, or their two sons, Gamal and Alaa. In this way, Mubarak hoped to preserve his family's privacy while also avoiding public criticism and claims of extravagant lifestyles. Even when his wife received her graduate degree, the media did not give the story much press coverage.

Starting in 1984, Mubarak also improved Egypt's relations with the Soviet Union, trying to mend the gap that had formed as a result of Sadat's earlier ousting of the Soviets. At the same time, Mubarak was careful not to anger or arouse the suspicions of the United States, which was (and remains) the primary source of financial aid and support for Egypt.

Mubarak also worked to restore public faith in a democratic system. In May 1980, Sadat had arranged for a constitutional amendment to be passed that would make him president for life, thereby doing away with the need for elections. He had also banned all parties except for his National Democratic Party (NDP, formerly the Arab Socialist Union). Mubarak allowed political parties to reemerge and reorganize themselves. During the 1984 elections for Parliament, six parties, including the Wafd, the NDP, the Society of Muslim Brothers, and others were represented. John Solecki wrote that, despite allegations of corruption, the election was fair: "For the first time ever, all 5 opposition parties were allotted 40 minutes each on state-run radio and television stations to outline their platforms in public. The government also let the parties hold election rallies in support of their candidates." The overwhelming winner in the election, however, was the party of Mubarak, the NDP.

The fact that the Society of Muslim Brothers had been permitted to participate in the elections was a significant step, as the group had been silenced under Nasser (it had tried to assassinate him in 1954). The Society of Muslim Brothers had been put down under Sadat as well, although Sadat also eventually encouraged the emergence of some fundamentalist groups as a tool for silencing his other critics. Thus, while the Society of Muslim Brothers had a violent past, it began working within the existing political system starting with the 1984 elections. However, the dramatic rise of other Islamic fundamentalist groups that were not working within the political system would pose the most significant challenge to Mubarak's presidency. Some of these groups (as witnessed by the assassination of Sadat) opted to use violence to spread their political message.

7

Challenges to Mubarak

THOUGH THE 1984 ELECTIONS WERE OPEN AND PRESENTED AN IMAGE OF Hosni Mubarak as a liberal, pro-democratic leader, the political system soon closed down again as the new president sought to protect his powers. The challenges to his authority and to the stability of his new government were, indeed, overwhelming and significant ones.

In 1985, the *Achille Lauro* hijacking commanded the world's attention. In October of that year, Israel bombed the headquarters of the Palestine Liberation Organization (PLO) near Tunisia, killing 69 people. Days later, Palestinians retaliated by hijacking the *Achille Lauro*, an Italian cruise ship sailing off the Egyptian coast and carrying more than 450 passengers. The hijackers also killed an elderly American passenger. After intense negotiations, the hijackers agreed to surrender to the Egyptian authorities, but the United States wanted to take them into its own custody. Mubarak knew that turning the four

Palestinians over to the Americans would upset his own people as well as other Arabs in the region.

His plan was to take the hijackers into Egyptian custody and then secretly fly them to Tunis so that the PLO leadership could decide their fate. On October 10, an Egyptian aircraft carrying the hijackers and Egyptian officials left Cairo, headed for Tunis. The American government was told that the hijackers had already left Egypt days earlier. However, American intelligence forces had been monitoring Mubarak's telephone conversations and knew about his bluff. They even knew the specific departure information of the jetliner. The American government commanded four U.S. fighter jets, which were stationed on a carrier in the Mediterranean, to surround the Egyptian jetliner and force it to land in Sicily. The hijackers were then turned over to the Italian authorities.

An embarrassed Mubarak called the American action "an act of piracy" and demanded an apology from President Ronald Reagan. Eventually, Reagan sent Mubarak an apologetic letter and Egyptian-American diplomatic tensions were smoothed over, but the incident further damaged the reputation of the United States in the region. Many Egyptians felt as they had in the British colonial era, when the nation was theoretically independent but helpless to curtail England's influence. Now, the American government had undermined the authority of the Egyptian president.

In 1986, Mubarak faced an even more dangerous situation on home soil. The soldiers who served in the Central Security Forces (CSF) were outraged in February of that year to discover that their term of service had been extended from three years to four. According to John Solecki in *Husni Mubarak*,

> The CSF, the worst treated and lowest paid of all Egypt's armed forces, is composed primarily of young men recruited from peasant villages; their main job is guarding foreign embassies and major government buildings in the cities.

In 1985, four men from the Palestinian Liberation Front (PLF) hijacked the *Achille Lauro*, an Italian passenger liner cruising off Egypt. The hijackers, who demanded the release of 50 Palestinians from an Israeli prison, killed 69-year-old, disabled American passenger Leon Klinghoffer. Klinghoffer's widow, Marilyn, *(center)* was the first of the former hostages to be escorted off the *Achille Lauro*.

When they found out about the extensions, 17,000 members of the CSF rioted on February 25, burning and looting in the tourist area of the Pyramids near Cairo. They then attacked Cairo itself, surging into the city. At that point, the rioters' composition and agendas changed. The CSF soldiers found themselves joined by young Islamic fundamentalists, who made it a point to attack establishments that sold alcohol (which is forbidden according to Islamic law). Before long, the riots spread to the Cairene suburbs and other nearby cities, and they were an assault on the authority of the Mubarak administration.

The government frantically tried to restore order. It imposed martial law and heavy curfews on the region. Gunfights

Mubarak was well aware that a similar situation could occur in Egypt, where the popularity of fundamentalist groups kept steadily increasing.

frequently broke out on the streets between the rioters and the Egyptian military forces that had been sent in to restore order. After three days, 107 deaths, and almost 4,000 arrests, the military was finally able to bring the riots under control. However, the Mubarak administration was terribly shaken by the incident, which had severely challenged its power and stability.

The event also made it clear to Hosni Mubarak that Islamic fundamentalism was a force to be reckoned with. According to William L. Cleveland in *A History of the Modern Middle East*, "In the years since 1979 [the years of the Islamic revolution in Iran] political Islam has spread well beyond the borders of Iran and has become one of the most enduring Middle Eastern phenomena of the last thirty years." In Iran, Cleveland wrote, "Radical political Islam achieved its first victory" by ousting a secular, pro-Western government. Mubarak was well aware that a similar situation could occur in Egypt, where the popularity of fundamentalist groups steadily increased.

As a result, Mubarak decided to keep in place the Emergency Laws that had been reimposed after Sadat's assassination. These laws, which are renewed annually or every three years, allow the government to arrest large numbers of people without charging them, as well as other actions that are essentially in violation of the Egyptian constitution because they violate human rights. Mubarak also took the interesting step of not naming a vice president. This unique move has intrigued many, who speculate that it is Mubarak's way of preventing a potential challenger to his authority. Others speculate that he is actually grooming one of his sons for the presidency, although his

Pope Shenouda III of the Coptic Orthodox Church sits for the photograph above on August 20, 1989. On September 3, 1981, Egyptian president Anwar Sadat ordered Pope Shenouda III into exile. In 1985, more than three years after Anwar Sadat's assassination, Hosni Mubarak released Pope Shenouda from exile, but he sentenced him to house arrest for more than three years.

insistence on his family's low public profile and privacy makes this explanation doubtful.

The problem for Mubarak of the rise of Islamic fundamentalism continued to intensify, as fundamentalists called for an Islamic government run by Islamic law. Mubarak, however, insisted on a secular government. "I am a religious man, but not an extremist," he once said. "I am a very moderate religious man." But the fundamentalists gained strength due to the fact that they offered faith as a solution for the problems many average Egyptians faced, especially that of poverty. Because the government failed to effectively boost the economy, the people were swayed by the message that the fundamentalists offered—that only by abiding by a strict Islamic code of living would social and financial prosperity be restored. People suffered, in other words, because society has strayed from the path of morality and righteousness. Furthermore, secular leaders were corrupt, while Islamic leaders were incorruptible, the fundamentalist message claimed.

The surge in Islamic fundamentalism caused another problem in Egypt. Egypt is a multifaceted society, in which the Coptic Christian population plays a significant and historic role. In the past, Copts and Muslims united to struggle for common causes, such as the frustration with British colonialism and the drive for independence in the earlier part of the century. However, the rise in Islamic fundamentalism sparked flames of hostility between the Muslim and Christian communities, especially as the Copts realized their vulnerability as a minority. The emphasis by the fundamentalists on an Islamic government and Islamic society could lead to persecution and oppression of non-Muslims, the Copts feared.

Their fear did not lack a rational basis. Toward the end of his life, in 1981, Anwar Sadat had imprisoned Pope Shenouda, the Coptic spiritual leader, because of the fighting that had broken out between Copts and Muslims. Many also say that Sadat wanted the pope to authorize pilgrimages of Copts to Jerusalem, as a way of gaining the favor of the Israelis after the Egyptian-Israeli peace treaty; the pope refused and thus angered Sadat. Pope Shenouda, a long-time social and human-rights advocate, was imprisoned in a monastery in the desert, which outraged the Coptic community. Copts hoped the pope would be released when Mubarak became president, but they were disappointed. Mubarak had Pope Shenouda released from his confinement in the desert but kept him under house arrest for three more years. Pope Shenouda was finally released on January 6, 1985, on the eve of the Coptic Christmas holiday. The tension between the Copts and Muslims would continue to be another manifestation of Islamic fundamentalism, but one that Mubarak took only hesitant steps to rectify.

8

The Gulf War and Egypt's Role

IN 1990, ANOTHER SITUATION AROSE THAT WOULD BRING THE CHALLENGE of Islamic fundamentalism and Egypt's relationship with and dependency on the West to the forefront. On August 2, 1990, Iraq, under President Saddam Hussein, invaded its southern neighbor, the tiny Persian Gulf nation of Kuwait. Because the attack came as a surprise and because Kuwait's armed forces were no match for the well-trained, expansive Iraqi military, the invasion of Kuwait was completed quickly and efficiently, and the country was annexed by Iraq in less than one week.

Iraq cited many reasons for the invasion, one of the first times in modern Middle Eastern history in which one Arab nation attacked another: Iraq was angry that Kuwait would not forgive a debt it had incurred during its decade of war with Iran, and Kuwait was allegedly drilling illegally in the Rumeila oil fields, thus stealing Iraqi oil. There was also an argument based on the fact that Kuwait had historically been part of Iraq; since Kuwait had been established by the British in 1923 to control Iraqi coastal access, Hussein claimed that Kuwait was and should remain a part of Iraq. Furthermore, by annexing Kuwait, Iraq solved a major problem: boosting its economy by opening more access to the Persian Gulf.

Saddam Hussein's invasion and annexation of Kuwait prompted a powerful response from the United States. The U.S. government feared that Iraq might then set its sights on Saudi Arabia as well, thus upsetting U.S.–Saudi relations and affecting oil prices. Under President George H.W. Bush, the United States launched Operation Desert Shield in the fall of 1990 and sent American troops to Saudi Arabia, at the invitation of the Saudi government. The United States also gathered international support—most importantly from Britain, France, and the Soviet Union—for its impending attack on Iraq.

It was essential for the United States to garner support from other Arab nations as well. Most Arab nations had disapproved of Saddam Hussein's attack on a neighboring Arab state (indeed, the Arab League strongly condemned the invasion), but they were, at the same time, reluctant to lend support to a Western-led attack on an Arab state. The United States used its financial muscle to rescue its cause: Egypt agreed to support an attack on Iraq and sent troops to join the coalition forces; in return, the United States forgave $7 billion of debt that it was owed by Egypt.

The war began on January 16, 1991. Known as Operation Desert Storm, it commenced as a series of lightning air strikes over Iraq. The air attacks destroyed the Iraqi infrastructure. It was also a major media event; for more than 40 days and nights, television news media covered the air strikes and broadcast them all over the world. In the Arab world, people were shocked and outraged by the sight of bombs and missiles lighting up the night skies over Iraqi cities, especially when it was later revealed that those bombs frequently missed military targets and hit civilian

Refugees are photographed following the Kuwaiti invasion. Egypt joined with U.S. forces in their fight against Iraq.

ones. On February 27, U.S. forces declared victory in Iraq, only a few days after a successful ground war had been put into effect and the Iraqi army was defeated.

In Egypt, people resented Hosni Mubarak for involving the army against another Arab country, especially as part of a Western coalition. Comparisons were drawn between Mubarak and Sadat, who had also been seen as sacrificing Egyptian independence to court the favor of the United States. It became clear that Egyptian foreign policy was being dictated by the American government because of the massive amount of financial aid it extended.

The 1991 Gulf War, and Egypt's support of the U.S.-led coalition, again affected Egypt's status in the Arab world. Under Gamal Abdel Nasser, Egypt had been a leader among the Arab nations, a position that had been lost under Sadat's presidency.

Egyptian soldiers fight against the Iraqi army during the last phase of the Gulf War. Amid much controversy, Egypt joined forces with the United States against Iraq during the 1990 Gulf War and was rewarded financially for the alliance.

Mubarak, however, had worked steadfastly during the 1980s to restore Egypt's status; due to careful, persistent diplomatic efforts, Egypt had been readmitted to the Arab League in 1989. Eventually, the Arab League even voted to return its headquarters to its original home: Cairo. After the Gulf War, however, Egypt's role was once again tarnished.

Within Egyptian society, the defeat of Iraq and Egypt's involvement lent credence and energy to the burgeoning radical Islamic movement. In 1992, a major insurgency movement erupted against the government, sparked by groups of young Islamic militants who clashed with police and security forces. Members of the police force and some government officials were targeted and murdered by the insurgents. The revolt caused a massive response on the part of the Mubarak administration, causing the president to clamp down on dissent. Mubarak began shifting his leadership style to Anwar Sadat's model, in order to protect his power. Historian William L. Cleveland wrote that, in the decade of the 1990s,

> Mubarak cast aside the liberalizing tendencies of his early presidency in favor of one-party, one-man rule. The government restructured the election laws to ensure that no popularly supported opposition parties could win seats in the People's Assembly.

In terms of dealing with the insurgents, arrests were carried out, and not only suspected insurgents, but also their friends and families, were incarcerated in what Cleveland described as "a campaign of intimidation and government violence that made no pretense of observing human rights and the rule of law."

The loss of a sense of a democratic political system and the new policy of silencing political dissidents hastened a sense of despair in Egypt, in which people felt that their democratic future was lost.

9

Decreasing Popularity

ON THE MORNING OF OCTOBER 12, 1992, A MAJOR EARTHQUAKE MEASURING
5.8 on the Richter scale racked the city of Cairo. Hundreds of
Cairenes died, and many more were injured. More than 200
buildings collapsed and thousands sustained severe damage.
The overall damages to the city's infrastructure caused by the
quake would cost billions to repair. Cairenes called on the government for help and relief amid the devastation, but the government's resources were stretched thin. Instead, the Society of
Muslim Brothers carried out its own relief campaign.

For years, the Society of Muslim Brothers had attempted
to change its image and had thus distanced itself from the
violent tendencies of other Islamic radical groups. In fact, the
society had been carrying out what William L. Cleveland called
a "quiet revolution." In other words, it had been attempting a
new strategy: breaking from the violent methods of its past
in order to work within the political system. Furthermore,

In October 1992, a devastating earthquake struck Egypt, leaving many people dead, injured, or homeless. Victims of the earthquake are photographed outside of the tents at the El Aiyat camp.

in its campaign to establish an Islamic government in Egypt, the Society of Muslim Brothers offered an alternative to the Egyptian people by offering social services such as education and welfare. These services were well run and meticulously organized, reaching and benefiting a large number of people. This strategy proved wildly successful and popular, especially in light of the government's obvious inability to cope with the growing population and staggering poverty.

After the 1992 earthquake, the Society of Muslim Brothers had an opportunity to display its organization and ability. It reacted quickly in the quake's aftermath to provide relief and medical services to afflicted people. The contrast between its

Mubarak aggressively suppressed the radical Islamists, often violating their human rights.

quick reaction and the slow one of the government was clear and helped boost the reputation of the Society of Muslim Brothers.

Thus, two forces of Islamic movements were growing within Egypt: a more radical one and one willing to hold a "quiet revolution." Historian Glenn Perry noted in *The History of Egypt* that Mubarak's regime adopted a two-pronged approach toward dealing with the two distinct movements, both dedicated to eradicating his secular government. Mubarak aggressively suppressed the radical Islamists, often violating their human rights. At the same time, he encouraged the rapid growth of Islam in Egyptian society, often supporting the out-pouring of religious sentiment in order not to appear opposed to this growing constituency.

Unlike Sadat, who tried to appear pious by using his given first name, Muhammad, rather than Anwar, Mubarak (whose real first name is also Muhammad) did not do that. However, he did promote a more conservative Islamic social agenda. Islamic clergy and leaders who supported Mubarak began to preach and speak in support of his administration, no doubt under the request of Mubarak himself. Furthermore, the court system became more conservative as well, seemingly to appease the growing conservative elements in the Egyptian population.

In 1995, the Egyptian courts found that Nasr Hamid Abu Zayd, a university professor and leading Egyptian intellec-tual, held anti-Islamic views, which made him an apostate. The courts ordered that his marriage to his wife be dissolved because he could not remain married to a Muslim while hold-ing his views. The couple fled the country to live in exile and are currently trying to have the court decision changed.

In another famous court case, the judiciary threatened to force the divorce of Egyptian feminist Nawal al-Sa'dawi. Al-Sa'dawi, a medical doctor by profession, is a leading activist for women's rights, and several of her books have made her famous, both in her native country and on an international level. She was charged in 2001 with making comments during a newspaper interview that criticized Islamic traditions. Her accusers alleged she was an apostate and could not be married to a Muslim. A legal attempt was made to force her to divorce her husband, Sherif Hetata. The court case shocked many people because, if successful, it would set a powerful precedent for the courts to interfere in the personal lives of Egyptians on the basis of religion. However, the court decision, handed down in 2001 by the Cairo Personal Status Court, eventually decided in favor of allowing al-Sa'dawi to remain married.

On June 26, 1995, Mubarak's increasing unpopularity became clear. There was an assassination attempt on his life during a visit to the city of Addis Ababa in Ethiopia. Mubarak and his entourage were driving through the streets of the city, on their way to an official meeting of the Organisation of African Unity. Suddenly, a van blocked the path of the motorcade. The van was stocked with explosives, and it succeeded in halting the motorcade enough to allow Islamic militants who were positioned on nearby rooftops to open fire on his limousine. Ten bullets hit the car, and two guards on motorcycle were killed, but Mubarak escaped without injury. He returned immediately to Egypt.

Later, Mubarak accused the Sudanese government of being involved in the plot to assassinate him. He said that Sudanese president Omar Hassan al-Bashir was a "secretary" to Dr. Hassan al-Turabi, the leader of Sudan's National Islamic Front. Egyptian officials also accused Ethiopian officials of being complicit in the plans, but they denied the charges. A few days after the assassination attempt, a raid was conducted by Ethiopian police on a house in which suspects in the attack were staying.

Several were killed during the raid, and Ethiopians claimed that those suspects were actually Egyptian nationals, not Ethiopians or Sudanese. Sudanese held anti-Egyptian demonstrations, angered over the accusations. Still, the Egyptian government held Sudan responsible.

For decades, there had been a bitter feud between Sudan and Egypt. Sudan, under President Jaafar al-Nimeiri, had been one of the few Arab countries to support Anwar Sadat's decision to make peace with Israel. However, al-Nimeiri was overthrown in 1985, and he was granted political asylum by President Mubarak. The new Sudanese government insisted that al-Nimeiri be extradited back to Sudan, but Egypt refused to turn him over. Thus, Sudan accused Egypt of supporting opposition forces. Relations became even worse when the Sudanese government was again overthrown by a coup led by Omar Hassan Ahmad al-Bashir. Al-Bashir established the Revolutionary Command Council for National Salvation, whose aim was to impose Islamic law on Sudan, including on the largely non-Muslim southern Sudanese population. Under al-Bashir, Sudan supported and allowed Egyptian Islamic militants who were wanted in Egypt to live in the country. Now Mubarak faced the challenge of living with a hostile neighbor.

In addition to the attempt on his life, Mubarak's failure to win the support of those Egyptians sympathetic to the Islamist movements was demonstrated by the murders of foreign tourists at Luxor in 1997. The fact that foreigners were attacked was meant to send a message to Mubarak's administration: The radical Islamic movement did not approve of his friendly relationship with the West and his secular government.

Furthermore, this movement did not approve of Egypt's continued peace agreement with the state of Israel. By April 1982, Israel had completely withdrawn from the Sinai Peninsula, and, in March 1989, it had returned the city of Taba to Egyptian control. However, it continued to occupy the Palestinian land it had seized in the 1967 war. Despite the enduring peace that Sadat had initiated with Israel, Mubarak maintained a more frigid diplomatic relationship with Egypt's neighbor. When Israel invaded its northern Arab neighbor, Lebanon, in June 1982, Mubarak condemned the invasion and recalled the ambassador to Israel home to Egypt. Mubarak could not be more outspoken—because of the support the United States had for Israel, the Egyptian president could not take a stronger stand. As William Cleveland noted,

> Egypt, once the main confrontation state, stood on the sidelines while the Israeli military closed in on Beirut. Mubarak had no choice but to honor the peace treaty and thus preserve Egypt's close relationship with the Unites States and the generous economic assistance it brought.

In September of 1999, another attempt was made on Mubarak's life in Egypt. While he was traveling through Port Said, waving from his car window, a man jumped out of the crowd, hurdled the barricade, and tried to stab him through the car's open window with a sharp object. Mubarak's arm was slightly injured, but his guards apprehended the would-be assassin before he could inflict further damage. One guard was hit by a stray bullet when the other guards fired on the attacker.

Mubarak's dependency on U.S. economic assistance also became clear during the second Gulf War on Iraq. The 1991 Gulf War had seen the military defeat of Iraq, but it had stopped short of removing Saddam Hussein from power. In 2002, U.S. president George W. Bush, the son of former president George H.W. Bush, alleged that Iraq was developing "weapons of mass destruction." Bush and his administration argued that Iraq could place those weapons in the hands of terrorist groups like al Qaeda, which had claimed responsibility for the terrorist attacks on the United States on September 11, 2001. Weapons inspection teams did not, however, uncover any evidence that Iraq was developing major weapons programs, which made it

Hosni Mubarak has survived no less than six assassination attempts. The photograph above was taken during the 1991 assassination attempt in Port Said, when a man approached the president's car with the intention to stab him.

difficult for the United States to garner international support, as it had during the 1991 war against Iraq. The only other major power that endorsed the effort was Great Britain, but notable criticisms came from former allies like France and Germany.

Like many other world leaders, Hosni Mubarak felt that a second war on Iraq was unjustified. In many countries around the world, protests and demonstrations against the impending war were mounted, and a very vocal antiwar movement emerged. Mubarak tried to convince the Bush administration not to pursue the planned course of action, but to no avail. Because the Emergency Laws were still in effect in Egypt, political demonstrations were banned. Mubarak's administration, however, allowed antiwar demonstrations to be staged, which many people believed represented a message from Mubarak to

George W. Bush. Once again, Mubarak could not condemn or oppose the war in harsher terms because it would mean risking the loss of the financial support Egypt received from the United States.

The second Gulf War on Iraq was launched on March 20, 2003. As part of what was called Operation Iraqi Freedom, U.S. and British forces attacked, and the forces of Saddam Hussein were defeated in only a few weeks. This was not surprising, since the Iraqi military and infrastructure had never recovered from the first Gulf War, 12 years earlier. The country had also been hindered by economic sanctions since then, which limited and put a great burden on its ability to prosper.

Mubarak's reputation hit an all-time low in Egypt. Many people resented the U.S.-led attack on Iraq, and they resented their president even more for his perceived silence and reluctance to criticize his biggest financial benefactor. In an effort to placate an angered and politically frustrated constituency, Mubarak opened up the political system slightly.

Iraq was occupied by U.S. and British forces, but it had fallen into chaos due to an insurgent rebellion, the kidnappings and murders of foreigners, and the assassinations of new government officials. In the midst of this, Mubarak announced that the September 2005 Egyptian elections would be open to the participation of other parties besides his own NDP. Previous elections in recent years, since Mubarak's suppression of opposition and dissent, had featured only Mubarak's name on voting ballots, and voters were asked to vote "yes" or "no." The changed policy would allow other candidates to run for the office of president.

The election, critics alleged, was still not set up fairly. For example, the Society of Muslim Brothers was still banned from participating (it has been forbidden in the past from even putting forth candidates for the People's Assembly but was able to do so by running candidates as independents). The Society of Muslim Brothers nevertheless encouraged Egyptians to vote but criticized Mubarak's campaign. "It is enough that he has been at the head of the authority for twenty-four years," said Mohammed Mahdi Akif, a spokesperson for the Society of Muslim Brothers, according to CFR.org, "during which he did not achieve political reform to make us support his candidacy." Others also alleged that the election would be unfairly run, since Mubarak's administration controlled the Egyptian media with an iron grip. How could anyone stand a chance to win, opponents argued, when Mubarak's image and campaign ads were broadcast all over billboards, television programs, and newspaper and radio spots? Such restrictions to media access for others hindered a free and fair election. Unsurprisingly, Mubarak was reelected by a vast majority.

10

Free Elections in Egypt

EGYPTIANS SOON GEARED UP FOR ANOTHER ROUND OF ELECTIONS, THOSE for the People's Assembly, held in November 2005, which Mubarak promised would also be free and open. Although 454 seats are available in the People's Assembly, all but approximately 30 of them were held by members of the NDP, Mubarak's party, because of past political oppression. Mubarak, however, promised that any party gaining at least 5 percent of the seats in the People's Assembly in the November elections could present candidates for the next presidential election in 2011, giving the parties several years to prepare a platform and organize their efforts.

The Society of Muslim Brothers was still not permitted to present candidates for the People's Assembly election, but it played a role indirectly by putting its support behind more than 150 independent candidates. People feared that the elections would be marred by corruption; thus, several organizations, including Amnesty International, the Egyptian Bar Association, the National Council for Human Rights, and other nongovernmental organizations announced their intentions to monitor the elections to ensure fairness and an open process.

The voting took place in rounds over the course of several weeks, and the candidates backed by the Society of Muslim Brothers surprisingly made significant gains in the earlier stages. Before long, it became clear that the Mubarak administration was becoming nervous, even though it was never in question that the NDP would win the majority of seats.

In early December, during the final round of voting, clashes broke out at voting polls between police officers and voters, especially in regions where the Society of Muslim Brothers commanded a lot of support. Voters alleged that police officers blocked them from getting to the polls and casting their ballots. In the ensuing violence, 12 people were killed and hundreds more suffered injuries. The Society of Muslim Brothers' leadership also alleged that more than 500 of its members had been arrested prior to the commencement of the elections to prevent them from participating. The allegations of corruption and manipulation gained credence by observations made by a panel of judges who monitored the elections. According to a BBC article titled "Violence Mars Egyptian Elections," Mahmoud al-Houderi, a spokesman for the judiciary panel, said, "We have witnessed in [some constituencies] the sealing off [of] polling stations to voters by police." He added, "Judges monitoring the stations have been prevented from opening them to let in voters."

Despite attempts to manipulate the election results, independent candidates did extremely well. Those backed by the Society of Muslim Brothers won a stunning 88 seats in the People's Assembly, increasing its previous presence sixfold, according to *Time* magazine reporter Scott MacLeod. The results officially made the banned Society of Muslim Brothers the main political challenge to Mubarak's administration.

Clashes erupt on December 7, 2005, as supporters of Egypt's government throw stones at supporters of Hosni Mubarak's opponents, the Muslim Brotherhood. Reports state that the police shot rubber bullets and tear gas at potential voters in areas with a strong Muslim Brotherhood population.

Is Egypt's political system finally opening up and becoming more democratic? Many historians and political experts doubt it. Although Mubarak seems to be loosening his control over the election process, many point to two facts. The first is that he still has never selected a vice president, despite many calls for him to do so. Perhaps he fears that a vice president would wrest too much control away from him by starting his own following and gaining support from his political party. In fact, for years, the minister of defense of Egypt was Muhammad Abd al-Halim Abu Ghazala. Abu Ghazala was considered to be the number-two man, second in control after Mubarak (he originally had been appointed to his post by Sadat but retained it after Mubarak assumed the presidency). He was also widely popular; he enjoyed tremendous respect within the party and the loyalty of many people. However, in 1989, Mubarak began to feel uncomfortable with Abu Ghazala so close to the seat of power, and he fired him from his role as minister of defense. Abu Ghazala was given a new job as an advisor to Mubarak, but his influence was greatly diminished.

The second fact is that Mubarak's eldest son, Gamal Mubarak, has become more well known on the political scene. Many expect that Mubarak is grooming his son to assume the presidency in the near future, which would certainly mar any pretense of a democratic Egypt. (A similar event recently took place in Syria, when Bashar al-Assad was named president after his father, long-ruling Hafiz al-Assad, died.) Gamal Mubarak, a graduate of the American University of Cairo, is a businessman in the banking industry. Unlike his father and the two previous Egyptian presidents, Nasser and Sadat, he has not pursued a career in the military. However, in recent years, he has become more involved with the National Democratic Party (NDP), perhaps to begin to build a base of support among its members. Hosni Mubarak actively denies that this succession will happen, emphasizing that Egypt already is a functioning democracy in which leaders are elected, but this prospect of Gamal as the next president continues to be a topic of discussion in many circles.

The future of true democracy under Mubarak looks grim for other reasons. For example, four of the judges who criticized the recent elections have been brought before a disciplinary tribunal; they refused to overlook the alleged fraud that took place, and they might face dismissal from their judicial posts as a result. (These four have also been very vocal in the past in advocating a bill that has been drafted but not officially made into law; the drafted bill allows the judicial branch of the government to be separated from the government's executive branch, which would allow it more autonomy and greater freedom.)

Gamal Mubarak, the president's youngest son, has been making a name for himself in the political world. In 2002, Gamal's father nominated him to become the general secretary of the Policy Committee. Many Egyptians are against Gamal's role in politics, arguing against inheritance of power.

Specifically, the four are being charged with accusing other judges of allowing electoral fraud to take place. By accusing fellow judges of behaving unethically, their critics claim that they have harmed the image of the judicial branch. Judges are normally granted immunity because they should have the freedom to be objective in their decisions without fear of reprisal, but the four were stripped of their immunity, making it possible to bring official charges against them in the case regarding electoral fraud. "I'm very appalled that they want to interrogate us for slander instead of investigating and questioning the judges who are accused of vote rigging," said Judge Hesham el-Bastawisy, one of the four judges on trial, to the Associated Press, according to Aljazeera.net. He added: "Everything we did and our goal is to defend the right of Egyptians to have independent, just judges that are not subject to the government, and for elections to be fair."

The trial comes amid a general call by many Egyptian judges for reform within the government. Furthermore, a rally held by citizens to show solidarity with the judges was broken up by the Egyptian police. The demonstrators were holding a meeting to protest the treatment of the judges when they were interrupted by hundreds of riot police. Officers then pulled 11 people out of the crowd and detained them, causing the angry demonstrators to chant "Down with Mubarak." The government was accused of suppressing free speech and silencing public dissent.

Muslim-Coptic tensions continue. In 2003, a play entitled *I Was Blind but Now I Can See* was performed in a Coptic church in Alexandria, Egypt. The plot centered on a poor young man who, out of financial desperation, converts to Islam because some Muslim men promise to reward him. However, he quickly experiences some dark aspects of his newfound religion and wants to become a Christian again, but the Muslim men threaten to hurt him if he does. The performance went largely unnoticed in the media, but someone had recorded it and began handing out DVDs of the performance. An article appeared in a local newspaper about the performance highlighting some aspects of the play that were allegedly offensive to Islam.

The newspaper article generated much talk and anger in Alexandria until approximately 3,000 Muslims held a protest demonstration outside the church. They demanded an apology not just from the church, but from Pope Shenouda himself. The Alexandrian police force was called to prevent the demonstrators from entering the church, and the situation was resolved peacefully.

A week later, however, a Muslim man stabbed a nun in the chest; she survived the attack, but tension between Muslims and Copts escalated. That same week, another demonstration was held outside the Coptic church. When police arrived, the situation quickly became violent because worshippers headed for Friday prayers at a nearby mosque were prevented from doing so. Instead, they performed their prayers in the street, then converged on the church and tried to storm it. Three protestors were killed and more than 100 people were arrested. The church's windows were smashed and much of the property damaged. Many shops and homes in the neighborhood also sustained damage, and the local residents, Muslim and Christian alike, were shocked and frightened.

Pope Shenouda joined Muslim clerics in calling for an end to the violence and a resumption of open dialogue, but the event seriously marred Muslim-Coptic relations. Furthermore, both communities accused the government of supporting the other community at the expense of their own.

In April 2006, a Coptic man was stabbed to death in a church in Alexandria. Two additional attacks took place simultaneously in other churches, sparking outrage from the Coptic community and riots that lasted for three days between Copts and Muslims. Most Muslims were shocked by the attacks, and it became clear that extremists were behind them, but Copts nevertheless felt that the government was not adequately protecting their community. People who attacked Copts had gotten away with light sentences for years, they charged, because the government was afraid to challenge the rising wave of Islamic fundamentalism. During the riots and demonstrations that followed the church attacks, many Copts marched while holding signs that questioned the government, such as "Hosni Mubarak, where are you?"

In recent years, terrorism has been a major problem in countries around the world. Egypt is no exception. It is now known that 5 of the 19 September 11 hijackers, including the ringleader, Mohammad Atta, were Egyptians. This fact has caused many problems for Egypt, as it depends on American foreign aid to sustain its troubled economy.

In Egypt, domestic acts of terrorism have also plagued the Mubarak administration, especially after the American-led attacks on Iraq during the second Gulf War. On October 7, 2004, a bomb blast rocked the Hilton Hotel in the resort city of Taba, on the Sinai Peninsula. A car bomb detonated when the car was driven and rammed into the side of the hotel. Hundreds of guests, mostly Israelis and Russians on vacation, were in the hotel, and many were injured. At least one other bomb was detonated nearby by a suicide bomber. The final death toll reached 34, most of them foreigners who were visiting the Red Sea resort town. The attack shocked many people, and al Qaeda, the group held responsible for the September 11, 2001 attacks on the United States, was thought to be behind the blasts.

In July 2005, a series of coordinated bomb blasts devastated the resort city of Sharm al-Sheikh in northern Egypt, killing more than 80 people. The most destructive of the three blasts occurred when a suicide bomber plowed his bomb-laced car into the Ghazala Gardens Hotel. Most of the dead were Egyptians, but many were also foreigners and tourists on vacation. President Mubarak made a forceful statement, calling the attacks "cowardly" and adding that "our battle with terrorism will continue with all the strength, resolve and will that we have." Indeed, several people were rounded up and interrogated after the attacks, but few thought that justice had really been served or that Egypt was totally safe from further acts of terrorism.

In April 2006, the Egyptian police force claimed to have struck a blow against terrorism when it arrested a number of men who were allegedly part of an underground terrorist cell called al-Taefa al-Mansura, or "Victorious Faction." The government accused the group of plotting a number of attacks against Coptic Christian sites as well as the Egyptian infrastructure, such as a gas pipeline.

On April 24, 2006, another devastating terrorist attack took place, again striking the tourism industry. A triple bombing struck the resort town of Dahab on the Sinai Peninsula. The attack killed 18 people, most of whom were Egyptians, and wounded dozens more. Dahab, which means "gold" in Arabic, is a much smaller resort than Taba or Sharm el-Sheikh, but its tourism base is strong. The bombing, however, threatened the future of the tourism industry, putting thousands of residents at risk of losing their livelihoods. Coptic Christians saw the attack as targeting their community, as it took place on the Coptic Easter holiday weekend. Many people across the Arab world condemned the bombings, emphasizing that the terrorists who were responsible for a string of attacks in the region were hurting only other Arabs. Fundamentalist organizations such as the Society of Muslim Brothers and Islamic Jihad also strongly condemned the terrorist acts.

Mubarak and his administration scrambled to portray the image that the government had the situation under control. In fact, 24 hours after the bombings, it was announced that Egyptian police had arrested at least 10 people suspected of being involved. However, two days after the attacks, suicide bombers attempted to attack international peacekeeping forces stationed in the northern part of the Sinai Peninsula; they managed only to blow up themselves and not injure anyone else.

The terrorist attacks occurring within Egypt are considered to be linked to Osama bin Laden's al Qaeda organization or with splinter groups loyal to or affiliated with al Qaeda. The purpose of the attacks is clear: to destabilize and overthrow Mubarak's government. They blame him for supporting the war on Iraq and for suppressing Islamic groups within Egypt. They also hold him responsible for Egypt's declining economy and high unemployment rate, which have left many Egyptians desperate.

Despite his attempts to wipe out corruption early in his presidency, Mubarak and his administration have been accused of succumbing to it in more recent years. This trend became very obvious during an incident that made the headlines in the world media. On February 3, 2006, an Egyptian ferry crossing the Red Sea sank. The *Al Salam Boccaccio 98*, operated by the El Salam Maritime Transport company, sank 50 miles (80 km) off the Egyptian coast. Carrying 1,400 passengers, mostly Egyptians, it had been making its way back to the city of Safaga, Egypt, from Duba, Saudi Arabia, when it sank.

Most of the Egyptians on board the ferry were employed in Saudi Arabia and were heading home for a visit. This fact is significant because the high rate of unemployment in Egypt, which has been estimated at 25 percent, has forced many citizens to seek work in other countries. The majority seek work in the oil-rich Arab gulf nations, where they work long hours for low pay, while the more educated elite seek work opportunities in the United States and Europe. (This has caused what some term a "brain drain," when the most educated Egyptians leave the country and take their talents elsewhere.)

The ferry disaster underscored this and other problems. Tensions increased at a rapid pace as the families of passengers waited for news of their fate. Anger mounted as the government did a poor job of managing information to the waiting family members in an efficient manner. People speculated about the cause of the sinking: Had it been another terrorist attack? Had there been a collision with another vessel? Within the first day after the sinking, as rescue teams searched the waters of the Red Sea, a few hundred survivors were located and saved.

Some of the survivors told a tale of horror: The ferry had apparently caught on fire, but the crew continued sailing

On February 3, 2006, the *Al Salam Boccaccio #98*, an Egyptian ferry carrying more than 1,400 people caught fire and sank off the coast of Egypt. In the photograph above, grieving relatives wait for returning survivors on the dock of Safaga Harbor. More than 1,000 people died in the sinking of the ferry.

toward Egypt for two hours before calling for help. An investigative report issued several months later claimed that as crew members sprayed water on the fire to extinguish it, water accumulated on the deck. The drain pipes on the deck, which should have drained the water, were blocked with debris, causing the accumulation. As water pooled on one side of the deck, the ferry became unstable, causing it to sink. Thus, the report stated, the blocked drains actually caused the disaster. Survivors testified that, as the crew sprayed water, passengers dived under the water and tried to unclog the drain, surfacing with pieces of paper and other trash. Their efforts were in vain, as more than 1,000 people died in the sinking, making it one of the deadliest maritime accidents in Egyptian history.

But the trouble was only beginning for the government. The investigation pointed the blame not only at the El Salam company, but at the government, which did not send out rescue teams until 10 hours after the ferry sank. The report especially accused the Egyptian Commission of Maritime Safety, which failed to conduct safety inspections. The ship was carrying forged documents, showing that the ship had met safety requirements when, actually, it had not. In fact, the ship was carrying more passengers that it should have been, and equipment such as lifeboats and fire extinguishers had fallen into disrepair and were in poor condition. The suspicion was that officials within the Egyptian Commission of Maritime Safety had been bribed by the owning company to allow the ferry to operate, despite not meeting the safety requirements. Such corruption was common in the Egyptian bureaucracy, but it had, in this instance, cost more than 1,000 innocent lives because of negligence and greed. The owner of the company, Mamdouh Ismail, who is also a member of Parliament, fled the country in the wake of the scandal and the fury that it sparked. Media reports highlighted the fact that Ismail enjoyed close contact with high-ranking officials in the government, which allegedly made it easier for his company to sidestep safety regulations.

The Egyptian people had grown tired of corruption, and Mubarak's administration was blamed for it. "The investigations showed that the operation of the ferry confirmed an excessive greed and willful desire to accumulate money, even at the expense of lives," the investigative report concluded.

Despite the relative political stability Egypt has enjoyed during Mubarak's tenure of almost 25 years, making him the longest-serving ruler of Egypt in two centuries, the country still suffers from a stagnating economy, high rates of unemployment, and mass poverty—all challenges that will have to be faced sooner rather than later.

CHRONOLOGY

A.D. 639	Islamic rule and Arabization of Egypt
1798	Napoleon Bonaparte invades Egypt, but is later ousted by British/Ottoman alliance
1869	Suez Canal opens
1875	Egyptian shares in Suez Canal sold to British government by Pasha Ismail due to bankruptcy
1882	British occupation of Egypt
1918	Wafd Party established
1919	Popular revolution calls for ousting of British
1928	Society of Muslim Brothers founded
1929	Hosni Mubarak born in Kafr-al-Meselha, Egypt
1936	British occupation ends; popular revolt of Palestinian Arabs against Zionism
1948	State of Israel established; first major Arab-Israeli war
1952	Free Officers overthrow King Faruq in a coup d'etat
1953	Egypt declared a free republic
1956	Gamal Abdel Nasser nationalizes Suez Canal
1958	Mubarak marries Suzanne Sabet
1961	"July Laws" establish Arab Socialist policy
1964	Mubarak enrolls at Frunze Military Academy; Palestine Liberation Organization (PLO) established
1967	Catastrophic defeat of Egypt and other Arab states in Arab-Israeli War
1970	Aswan High Dam project completed
1971	Nasser dies; Anwar Sadat becomes president

1972	Mubarak becomes commander in chief of the Egyptian Air Force
1973	Mubarak becomes a hero in the Yom Kippur War against Israel
1975	Mubarak selected to be Sadat's vice president
1977	Sadat visits Jerusalem and begins peace process
1978	Egypt ousted from the Arab League
1979	Camp David Accords signed between Egypt and Israel
1981	Sadat assassinated; Mubarak becomes new president of Egypt
1982	Israel evacuates its forces from Sinai Peninsula
1989	Israel returns Taba to Egypt
1990–1991	Iraq invades Kuwait; Egypt joins alliance to attack Iraq and protect Saudi Arabia
1992	Major earthquake devastates Cairo
1995	Assassination attempt on Mubarak's life
1997	Massacre of tourists at Luxor
2003	Egypt reluctantly participates in U.S.-led war on Iraq
2005	"Open" elections held in Egypt; Mubarak reelected

BIBLIOGRAPHY

BOOKS/ARTICLES

Cleveland, William L. *A History of the Modern Middle East.* New York: Westview Press, 2004.

Goldschmidt, Arthur, Jr. *Modern Egypt: The Formation of a Nation-State, Second edition.* New York: Westview Press, 2004.

MacLeod, Scott. "Look Who's Getting Votes." *Time.* December 19, 2005: p. 54.

Perry, Glenn. *The History of Egypt.* The Greenwood Histories of the Modern Nations Series. Westport, Conn.: Greenwood Press, 2004.

Solecki, John. *Husni Mubarak.* World Leaders, Past and Present Series. New York: Chelsea House, 1990.

WEB SITES

"Egypt Breaks Up Solidarity Rally." Al-Jazeera.net. April 27, 2006
http://english.aljazeera.net/NR/exeres/6A75AB36-B63B-4ED6-8093-862A634F93BF.htm.

"Egypt Breaks Up Terrorist Ring." BBC Online. April 19, 2006.
http://news.bbc.co.uk/2/hi/middle_east/4922658.stm.

"Egypt Church Attacks Spark Anger." BBC Online. April 15, 2006.
http://news.bbc.co.uk/2/hi/middle_east/4911346.stm.

"Egypt: Elections." Council on Foreign Relations. August 31, 2005.
http://www.cfr.org/publication/8744/egypt.html.

"Egypt Freezes Assets of Disaster Ferry Owner." Reuters News Agency. April 13, 2006.
http://za.today.reuters.com/news/NewsArticle.aspx?type=topNews&storyID=2006-04-13T122745Z_01_BAN344850_RTRIDST_0_OZATP-EGYPT-FERRY-20060413.XML.

"Egypt Struggles to Save Cairo's Islamic Heritage: Earthquake Shakes Response from International Experts to Crumbling Ancient Buildings." Christian Science Monitor. November 16, 1993.
Retrieved November 22, 2005 from ProQuest Direct Database.

"Egypt: The New Spectre of Terror." BBC Online. November 20, 1997.
http://www.news.bbc.co.uk/1/hi/world/analysis/32048.stm.

"Egyptian Tourist Massacre." BBC Online. November 17, 1997.
http://www.news.bbc.co.uk/1/hi/world/31958.stm.

Farag, Fatemah. "Shaken, Not Stirred." Al-Ahram Weekly. August 29–
September 4, 2002.
http://weekly.ahram.org.eg/2002/601/eg4.htm.

"Four Egyptian Judges in the Dock." Al-Jazeera.net. February 16, 2006.
http://english.aljazeera.net/NR/exeres/31C9F3CA-D4F2-4BE0-BE27-
73D51344B890.htm.

"1996: Greek Tourists Killed by Egyptian Gunmen." BBC Online. http://news.
bbc.co.uk/onthisday/hi/dates/stories/april/18/newsid_2525000/2525335.stm.

Noakes, Greg. "Egypt's Travails: Perilous Storms or Passing Squalls?" The
Washington Report on Middle East Affairs. July 31, 1996, Vol. 15(2): p. 61.
Retrieved November 22, 2005 from ProQuest Direct Database.

"Q&A: Egypt's Election Issues." BBC Online. December 1, 2005.
http://www.news.bbc.co.uk/2/hi/middle_east/4417204.stm.

"Security Tightened in Egypt After Massacre." CNN.com.
November 18, 1997.
http://www.cnn.com/WORLD/9711/18/egypt.attack.mubarak.

"Toll Climbs in Egyptian Attacks." BBC Online. July 23, 2005.
http://news.bbc.co.uk/1/hi/world/middle_east/4709491.stm.

"Violence Mars Egyptian Elections." BBC Online. December 1, 2005.
http://www.news.bbc.co.uk/2/hi/middle_east/4487128.stm.

Wakin, Daniel J. "Successor to Ancient Alexandria Library Dedicated." New
York Times. October 17, 2002: p. A14.
Retrieved November 22, 2005 from ProQuest Direct Database.

Wiseman, James. "Insight: The Death of Innocents: The Luxor Massacre."
Archaeology. March/April 1998, Vol. 51(2).
http://www.archaeology.org/9803/abstracts/insight.html.

FURTHER READING

BOOKS

Carlisle, Rodney P. *Persian Gulf War*. New York: Facts On File, 2003.

Harris, Geraldine. *Ancient Egypt, Third Edition*. New York: Chelsea House, 2007.

Subanthore, Aswin. *Egypt, Second Edition*. New York: Chelsea House, 2007.

Wagner, Heather Lehr. *Anwar Sadat and Menachem Begin*. New York: Chelsea House, 2007.

Wilson, Susan. *Egypt*. Milwaukee, Wisc.: Gareth Stevens Publishing, 1999.

WEB SITES

Egypt State Information Service.
http://www.sis.gov.eg/En/Default.htm

Hosni Mubarak.
CountryStudies.us. http://countrystudies.us/egypt/46.htm

Country Profile: Egypt. BBC Online.
http://news.bbc.co.uk/2/hi/middle_east/country_profiles/737642.stm

Photo Credits

page:

INDEX

ABOUT THE AUTHORS

SUSAN MUADDI DARRAJ is associate professor of English at Harford Community College in Bel Air, Maryland. She is the author of several biographies for Chelsea House, as well as the managing editor of the *Baltimore Review*.

ARTHUR M. SCHLESINGER, JR. is the leading American historian of our time. He won the Pulitzer Prize for his books *The Age of Jackson* (1945) and *A Thousand Days* (1965), which also won the National Book Award. Professor Schlesinger is the Albert Schweitzer Professor of the Humanities at the City University of New York and has been involved in several other Chelsea House projects, including the series *Revolutionary War Leaders*, *Colonial Leaders*, and *Your Government*.